BONSAI

SECRETS

BONSAI
SECRETS

Designing, growing, and caring for
your miniature masterpieces

PETER CHAN

The Reader's Digest Association, Inc.
Pleasantville, NY/Montreal/Sydney

CONTENTS

This edition published by The Reader's Digest Association Inc.
by arrangement with
THE IVY PRESS LIMITED
The Old Candlemakers
Lewes, East Sussex BN7 2NZ, U.K.

Text and design copyright © THE IVY PRESS LIMITED 2006

FOR IVY PRESS
Creative Director: Peter Bridgewater
Publisher: Sophie Collins
Editorial Director: Jason Hook
Art Director: Karl Shanahan
Senior Project Editor: Caroline Earle
Designer: Kevin Knight
Illustrations: Rhian Nest-James
Photography: Peter Chan & APM Studios

FOR READER'S DIGEST
U.S. Project Editor: Miranda Smith
Copy Editor: Marilyn Knowlton
Canadian Project Editor: Pamela Johnson
Project Designer: George McKeon
Executive Editor, Trade Publishing: Dolores York
President & Publisher, Books & Music: Harold Clarke

Library of Congress Cataloging-in-Publication Data

Chan, Peter.
   Bonsai secrets : designing, growing, and caring for your miniature masterpieces / Peter Chan.
      p. cm.
   ISBN 0-7621-0624-7 (pbk.)
   1. Bonsai. I. Title.

   SB433.5.C43 2006
   635.9'772--dc22

                                    2005051043

ISBN: 0-7621-0624-7 (paperback)
ISBN: 0-7621-0568-2 (hardcover)

Address any comments about Bonsai Secrets to:

The Reader's Digest Association, Inc.
Adult Trade Publishing
Reader's Digest Road
Pleasantville, NY 10570-7000

For more Reader's Digest products and information,
visit our website:
www.rd.com (in the United States)
www.readersdigest.ca (in Canada)
www.readersdigest.com.au (in Australia)

Printed in China

1 3 5 7 9 10 8 6 4 2

INTRODUCTION

The art of bonsai has always been shrouded in mystery. When the European explorers and plant hunters of the 17th century first stumbled upon these curious trees in the imperial palaces of China and the Shogun castles of Japan, they had no idea what to make of them. These perfectly formed, miniature replicas of apparently full-grown trees posed an enigma: Had they been grown from seed that was somehow genetically altered, or were these exquisite creations a different species of plant altogether?

 For nearly 1,700 years, from its conception as an art form in China during the Qin (Chin) dynasty (221–206 BCE), bonsai remained the quiet pastime of artists and scholars. Under the patronage of successive imperial dynasties, the creation and appreciation of bonsai was later taken up by the Chinese nobility and wealthy merchant classes and by the 7th century, bonsai was synonymous with high fashion. When the art of bonsai spread to Japan around the 12th century, its development followed the same pattern as in China.

Bonsai in the West

It was only after World War II that bonsai began to slip into Western consciousness. But even as other Eastern arts like kung-fu and karate were absorbed and became part of popular culture, bonsai held fast to its veil of secrecy. Why were bonsai trees so small, and what was the fascination of owning them? The practice provoked part fascination and part suspicion. Dwarf trees that seemed to defy nature suggested to some a dark, perhaps even cruel, art. The great bonsai masters, held in awe and high

Once you have mastered the techniques, creating a bonsai is about personal vision. Your trees should be an expression of yourself.

esteem in the East, allowed only a few privileged individuals into their inner circle and seldom divulged their secrets publicly. An esoteric practice that spawned inexplicable results, bonsai seemed the living embodiment of the inscrutability of the Orient. Even today, now that many of the old myths and prejudices of the past have been debunked, bonsai retains a sense of mystery. It is precisely this quality that attracts enthusiasts, particularly in the West. To create something of beauty and elegance from an ordinary tree or shrub is indeed awe-inspiring, but entirely possible. Through a combination of practical skill and insider knowledge—which I shall be sharing with you in this book— you, too, will be able to transform a natural, living plant into a bonsai that is the very expression of balance and tranquility.

In the last 30 or 40 years, there has been a huge surge of interest in bonsai in the West. Once an esoteric art with a few passionate devotees, bonsai is now firmly rooted in our gardening culture. Advances in air travel have made it much easier for bonsai dealers to import new plants, and the Internet has played a central role in bringing enthusiasts together. Bonsai's growing popularity is undoubtedly linked to the increasing intensity of modern life, to urbanization, and the desire of city dwellers to rediscover nature. As our leisure time becomes more precious and our living space more restricted, bonsai presents itself as the perfect solution. You can create an oasis of calm within a tiny apartment or a small courtyard and dedicate yourself for just a few minutes a day to a pastime that transports you away from the hassles of everyday life.

This group of trees looks so natural that it is hard to imagine that it was made by someone many years ago. Like all skills, bonsai can be learned, and with the help of insider secrets, you too should be able to create something this beautiful.

People find themselves drawn into the world of bonsai along many different routes. Some start off as gardeners; others become interested through an appreciation of Eastern arts such as literature or painting. In recent years, fashionable Eastern practices like t'ai chi and minimalist Zen aesthetics have attracted many more enthusiasts. My personal introduction to bonsai came through the study of ceramics, in the mid-1960s. Like everyone involved in the bonsai world, I fell in love with the Eastern aesthetic and the principles of Eastern philosophy that govern it. And with bonsai, there's the added fascination of watching living things grow.

Seasoned bonsai growers make the hobby look effortless and easy. When you see fine examples of bonsai, you may well wonder whether it will ever be possible to attain such high standards. What is the secret? This book can help you to achieve the same high standards. Expertise in bonsai requires patience and practice, but as with any art or craft, the techniques can be learned. Every skill, however complex—playing a beautiful piece of music or painting a watercolor—can be analyzed and broken down into more manageable steps. The step-by-step guides in this book are designed to help you build up your skill base gradually. In this book I have revealed a lifetime's worth of secrets, learned from other bonsai masters, from fellow enthusiasts, and through a long process of trial and error. The practical step-by-step approach will enable you, in time, to master the art for yourself and discover a few secrets of your own.

1

FIRST
PRINCIPLES

"The longest journey begins with the first step."

WHAT IS BONSAI?

The literal meaning of "bonsai" is simply a tree or shrub that grows in a pot. "Bon" or "poon"— depending on how you pronounce the Chinese character—means pot or container, while "sai" or "su" means tree. In Japanese, the word "bonsai" (pronounced "bone-sigh") is spelled using the same two Chinese characters because the ancient Japanese Kanji script has its basis in Chinese. But not every tree or shrub grown in a container can be regarded as a bonsai. There is much more to bonsai than meets the eye.

 So, what is it that distinguishes a bonsai tree from any other tree or shrub? A bonsai must have some kind of special quality about it to give it that particular "bonsai" character. The image that typically comes to mind is a small, gnarled-looking tree, with a twisted trunk and clouds of tight green foliage—planted in a ceramic pot. A bonsai should be a perfect miniature of the same tree fully grown in its native habitat. When viewing it, you should have the impression that you are looking through the wrong end of a telescope.

Key attributes

Bonsai are created from ordinary trees or shrubs. They are not grown from genetically modified seeds; nor are they a distinct species. If a bonsai is left to its own devices—i.e., not pruned regularly, and planted in the ground, not a pot—it will develop into an "ordinary," full-grown plant or tree.

In order to be a bonsai, a plant has to be miniature. The miniaturization process is achieved through a combination of pruning and the use of a pot to restrict root growth. A tree or shrub that is planted in the ground is not a bonsai. A bonsai may,

Two junipers of similar size. One is an untrained nursery shrub in a plastic pot, while the other has been pruned and shaped into a bonsai, complete with driftwood effects *(see page 47)* on a gnarled trunk and its branches wired in the right position.

in fact, be very large, because there is no limit to size—as long as it is in a container. In China, you see bonsai that are 10–15 feet (3–4.5 m) tall, grown in large pots. At the other extreme, some bonsai are barely 1 inch (2.5 cm) high, and the pots in which they are grown are no bigger than thimbles.

Bonsai often give the impression of great age, but a plant does not have to reach a certain age to qualify as a bonsai. Bonsai growers can use special techniques to create the illusion of age *(see pages 29 and 47)*. Sometimes a 10-year-old bonsai can be as striking as a 100-year-old specimen.

Above all, a bonsai must be a work of art. If it has no artistic merit, it is just an ordinary plant in a pot. The beauty of bonsai is that, unlike a painting or sculpture, it lives, breathes, grows, and changes—it is always a "work in progress."

When is a bonsai not a bonsai?

In the 1970s and 1980s, when bonsai was becoming more widely known in the West, many enterprising growers and nurseries sold young seedlings and cuttings that had hardly any shaping or styling, placed them in bonsai-style containers, and passed them off as genuine bonsai. These

SECRETS OF SUCCESS

In China and Japan, over the centuries, the art of bonsai was passed down to the ordinary people. The unsophisticated peasant farmers observed nature and created miniature versions of what they saw around them. One of the most valuable lessons they taught us is the art of pruning. It is the pruning and shaping process that makes each bonsai unique. You could say that bonsai is sophisticated topiary.

plants may have had the potential to become bonsai, but they cannot be regarded as bonsai in this state. In the bonsai fraternity, such plants are jokingly referred to as "sticks in pots."

You may also come across much older shrubs and trees with no shaping or training that have been simply planted in bonsai containers. They typically have no artistic merit and therefore don't qualify as bonsai. But because they can be used as raw material, bonsai hobbyists refer to these plants as potential bonsai, or "potensai" for short.

The tree on the left qualifies as a bonsai because it has all the essential ingredients— a gnarled old twisted trunk, a bit of driftwood *(see page 47)*, and the overall shape is very pleasing. The tree on the right has potential for the future, but has not developed enough maturity and styling.

ORIGINS

The origins of bonsai as a horticultural activity are lost in the mists of time. It is almost impossible to put a precise date on when it all began. What is known for certain, however, is that the art originated in China and not in Japan, as is often believed. By the time of the Tang dynasty in the early 7th century (618–907 CE), bonsai was very much in vogue in the homes of the Chinese nobility, as is shown by famous paintings of that period. By the Sung dynasty in the 10th century (960–1280 CE), bonsai had become an integral part of the social fabric.

 Some scholars believe that the cultivation of plants and flowers in China dates back as long as the Chinese civilization itself, some four millennia. Somewhere along the way, these ancient horticulturalists must have begun to experiment with using ceramic containers. Since many of the plants they grew in these pots were shrubs and trees, bonsai was the natural progression. Historical records point to the cultivation of "artistic pot plants" during the Jin (Chin) dynasty around the 3rd century (265–420 CE). These creations were bonsai in its most rudimentary form.

The cultivation of plants in pots was not the exclusive preserve of the Chinese civilization. There are paintings in Egyptian pyramids that depict plants growing in stone containers. In India, the practitioners of Ayurvedic medicine often traveled around the country carrying medicinal plants and herbs that were grown in little pots. This way they always had them handy to use as remedies for various ailments. However, no records exist of plants being deliberately miniaturized for artistic purposes other than in China.

Mysticism

Bonsai was given a mystical dimension through its association in China with the early Taoist priests. The priests viewed miniaturization as a way of distilling and concentrating magical qualities in a compact object. Obsessed with achieving immortality, they also believed that by dwarfing a tree, they could slow down the rate at which the sap would flow in the same way that slowing down someone's heart and pulse was seen as a means of prolonging human life.

The ancient monks and sages devoted a great deal of effort to researching miniaturization techniques. Plants and trees were satisfying subjects on which to experiment because keeping them in containers for prolonged periods invariably succeeded in controlling their growth. The general public, however, perceived this effect as something extraordinary. The common belief was that anyone who could miniaturize plants must possess magical powers. People also believed that the dwarfed trees themselves were supernatural.

In ancient times, bonsai trees and the bonsai masters who worked on them were thought to possess supernatural powers.

The shapes of individual bonsai trees in Chinese style are reminiscent of the trees depicted in traditional Chinese paintings. Some commentators would say that the images in the paintings resemble bonsai trees, but in fact it is the trees in the paintings that have influenced the shapes of Chinese bonsai.

The fact that many bonsai bore resemblance to the gnarled old masters who created them only added to the mystique. In fact, the miniaturization process is a mechanical one: a combination of pruning and shaping. The artists who do it well are recognized as having exceptional skill and artistic ability, rather than unworldly powers. But let's not strip it of its magic altogether. When you stand in front of a perfect specimen, and it takes your breath away with its beauty, it is easy to believe, like those Chinese monks of ancient times, that a bonsai does have some inherent magical quality. However, the real magic of bonsai is achieved through patience, dedication, and the careful application of techniques—all of which can be learned.

WHAT IS PEN-JING?

From very early times, the great emperors of China surrounded their palaces with lakes and ponds, artificial hills and mountains that were small-scale replicas of the geographical features found in the kingdom. This form of gardening evolved into the practice of "pen-jing," or potted tray landscapes. The ancient Chinese pen-jing masters created entire landscapes in miniature using trees, plants, rocks, figurines, and models of people, pagodas, and bridges—all within the confines of a single container. In "pun-choi," or ordinary bonsai, the bonsai artist focuses his attention on an individual tree rather than on creating a miniature landscape. Bonsai, as we know it today, is based on this approach.

THE SPREAD OF BONSAI

The Chinese civilization has always been a major influence on Japanese life and culture. For almost 1,000 years, from the 6th century CE, Japan imported everything from Zen Buddhism to calligraphy from its neighbor. The Japanese sent countless delegations to China to find out more about the language, literature, customs, and also the arts and crafts. One such import was bonsai.

The Japanese have always been reluctant to acknowledge that bonsai was introduced to Japan from China. Japanese bonsai books and bonsai masters simply state that bonsai is a traditional Japanese art, which can be traced back to the Kamakura period during the late 12th century CE. In fact, the Chinese style of bonsai *(see box opposite)* was in vogue in Japan up to the early 20th century. It is only in more modern times that a distinctive Japanese style of bonsai has emerged. Its influence has been such that most Westerners believe that bonsai is a Japanese art.

Bonsai in the West

The plant hunters from Britain, France, and Holland who accompanied the trading missions to China and Japan in the mid-17th century were naturally intrigued by the examples of bonsai that they found. However, although some bonsai were inevitably brought back to Europe, hardly any survived the long sea journeys. It wasn't until the late 19th century that bonsai were shown in mainland Europe, at the Paris International Exhibitions of 1878 and 1889. The British public had to wait until the 1909 London Imperial International Exhibition for their first glimpse.

A Japanese bonsai master in the 1920s enjoying his trees. The bonsai of that era were mostly in the Chinese style. It is only in the last 70 years that a distinct Japanese style of bonsai has emerged.

CHINESE BONSAI

Many different schools of bonsai have evolved in China over the centuries, but each school recognizes two broad genres—miniature potted landscapes (pen-jing) and individual miniature trees. The most well-known Chinese schools are the Southern, or Lingnan school, and the Northern, or Suzhou school.

SOUTHERN, OR LINGNAN, SCHOOL

Followers of the Southern, or Lingnan School, practice the "clip and grow" method of styling. Lingnan bonsai are stylized and formal, and the trunks all tend to be slender in relation to tree height. Markedly different from contemporary Japanese bonsai, these plants can look unnatural and, as such, are an acquired taste in the West.

NORTHERN, OR SUZHOU, SCHOOL

The bonsai of the Northern, or Suzhou, School more closely resemble the bonsai you come across in Japan, with which we are more familiar in the West. The Chinese, of course, say that Japanese-style bonsai is heavily influenced by the Suzhou school.

CONTEMPORARY CHINESE BONSAI

Chinese bonsai is still largely based on the potted landscape concept, which is not currently fashionable elsewhere in the world.

Although this Chinese juniper bonsai is in the Japanese style, it strongly resembles some of the bonsai made in the Shanghai area of China. But as long as the tree is beautiful, its actual style is of little consequence.

These appearances didn't cause much of a stir. There was little or no interest in bonsai for the next four decades. It was only after World War II and the U.S. occupation of Japan that a more widespread interest in bonsai began to take hold. Many U.S. servicemen had come across bonsai during their time in Japan and took their interest back home. The Japanese immigrant population on the west coast of the United States and in Hawaii also helped spread interest in the art form.

During the 1950s and 1960s, bonsai became more widely known, and specialist clubs and societies began to form in Europe and America. As the Western fascination with Eastern culture grew, so did the interest in bonsai. The next two decades saw an explosion of bonsai as a hobby in every corner of the globe.

Behind the Bamboo Curtain

But while interest in Japanese bonsai was flourishing in the West, interest in Chinese bonsai was not. The Cold War brought with it not only the Iron Curtain but also the Bamboo Curtain. The West was suspicious of anything to do with Communism, and consequently, China was a closed country for nearly three decades, from 1949 to the late 1970s. The internal upheaval of the Chinese Cultural Revolution during the 1960s and 1970s did nothing to encourage the art of bonsai, which was frowned upon as a bourgeois pastime.

Fortunately, political situations and attitudes change. Bonsai is now recognized in China as an important trade commodity. Through export trade and tourism, Chinese-style bonsai currently enjoys a high level of exposure.

RELIGION

Many people believe that because bonsai originated in the Far East, where the great religions of Taoism, Confucianism, and Buddhism have their roots, bonsai must carry religious significance. Indeed, many temples house fine collections of bonsai, which are displayed as decorative features in order to enhance the surroundings and to create the appropriate ambience for worship and meditation. But is there a deeper meaning to bonsai than just the decorative aspect?

 Although there is no overt link between bonsai and religion, the sublime beauty of a prize bonsai has an innate spirituality, and is a manifestation of some of the qualities that the Eastern religions espouse. Respect for nature and the appreciation of its beauty are integral to Eastern philosophy. The importance of balance, which is essential to the health and aesthetic of a tree, is also stressed.

A common theme that runs through all the Eastern religions is nature as a manifestation of the divine. When you create a bonsai, you are in some way trying to mimic the natural world. A bonsai is a poem to nature—an expression of our wonder at it and a distillation of its qualities.

Zen and bonsai

The cultivation and appreciation of bonsai is also a relaxing and holistic pastime, with the power to inspire and rejuvenate the human soul. This in itself has a spiritual significance.

Zen, or Chan, Buddhism was practiced originally by the Chinese and taken to Japan in the 8th century. It was in Japan that the Zen

These junipers clinging to a crag symbolize man's struggle for survival in the face of adversity—a common theme of bonsai folklore.

concepts were developed and taken to even greater heights by the Zen priests, who were also the great artists and literary scholars of the day. Bonsai aesthetics, in common with most of the Eastern arts, have been greatly influenced by Zen philosophy.

The twin concepts of "simplicity" and "austere sublimity," which lie at the very heart of Zen, find eloquent expression in the ink-wash paintings of the Chinese and the Sumi-e paintings of the Japanese. In these paintings, all nonessential elements are discarded, leaving only the core or essence to make a statement. Zen meditation works in a similar way, so that a person attains an enlightened state of mind by discarding all the inessential "baggage" that clutters their life, leaving only the things that really matter. In bonsai, trees are shaped and styled according to Zen principles. Anything that is surplus or irrelevant is discarded. In this approach, "less is more," and empty space is full of meaning. In the Literati, or Bunjin, style of bonsai *(see pages 55 and 111)*, which is a classic example of the Zen aesthetic, the shape and form are austere to the point of minimalism.

SECRETS OF SUCCESS

The essence of Japanese aesthetics, often expressed as "wabi" and "sabi" *(see pages 112–113)*, is deeply rooted in Zen philosophy. At the heart of the wabi-sabi concept, which would take a lifetime to understand fully, is the idea that the highest form of art embodies three essential characteristics: simplicity, naturalness, and tranquillity. These qualities manifest themselves in the design and creation of all successful bonsai.

The Zen dry landscape garden at Daito-kuji temple in Kyoto, Japan. The rocks symbolize the immortal isles, while the gravel represents the sea. Every culture creates great works of art as dedications to the divine. Art is often a symbolic expression of our religious ideas and sentiment.

THE ART OF BONSAI

Bonsai includes a combination of art and model-making, but at the heart of bonsai lies horticulture. You need to have some knowledge of plants in order to understand how bonsai grow and what each particular plant species needs to thrive. If a tree is not healthy, it cannot be beautiful. But the creation of a perfect miniature tree also involves artistic skill. Horticulture and art are both essential, and each has a vital contribution to make in the creation of a beautiful miniature tree.

 Bonsai creation is an unending quest for artistic perfection. As the tree grows and changes, you have to dedicate yourself to its health and well-being while also allowing it to develop as an artistic creation. It may sound like a lifetime of toil, but it is also what makes the art so fascinating. As you tend, respond to, and shape your bonsai, you forge a perfect symbiotic relationship with nature and become acutely attuned to the bonsai you have created.

It is possible to start out as a bonsai hobbyist without any previous knowledge of horticulture. The skills you need can be easily learned: bonsai horticulture is no more complicated than growing plants in containers. The difference is that bonsai involves pruning and shaping to give the plants that characteristic artistic quality.

To become a bonsai master takes a lifetime, and a true master never considers his or her knowledge complete. Part of the mystery of bonsai is that you never stop learning. Every tree is unique—each will grow differently and have its own needs and idiosyncrasies. Each time you prune your tree or wire a branch, you change the course of its development. Nature will make its own decisions, too. The inevitability of change is a central tenet of Buddhism. The fact that your tree can never be finished is part of the adventure and the mystery.

Needle juniper trees grown in the Raft style—that is, all the individual trees are connected by a common root. The composition is 37 inches (94 cm) high x 53 inches (1.3 m) wide.

SECRETS OF SUCCESS

Bonsai aesthetics are based largely on convention. Once you have grasped the basic principles *(see pages 48–51)* and are confident that you can keep a plant healthy, you will feel more free to experiment. An appreciation of the finer points of bonsai, such as shapes, styles, and choice of pot, will follow as your understanding develops.

A Japanese mountain maple, reputed to be more than 100 years old, that has been in the author's collection for the past 30 years. It looks quite different from its appearance three decades ago.

Pemphis acidula—a popular tropical species among Indonesian bonsai enthusiasts. This is grown in the Literati style.

2

CHOOSING A BONSAI

"Choice is a very personal thing—we should recognize that everyone has different tastes."

INDOOR OR OUTDOOR?

Before you set out to discover more about bonsai, you probably had a mental image of a tree no more than a foot (30 cm) or so high, placed on an office desk or a side table in a living room. One of the most common misconceptions about bonsai is that they can only be grown successfully indoors. This is the popular view of bonsai, but it isn't entirely correct. In fact, although some bonsai are specifically intended to be kept inside, the majority of bonsai are outdoor species.

 Indoor bonsai were developed by the horticultural industry to meet the demand for bonsai that could be kept in the home. Traditional bonsai enthusiasts have always treated these bonsai as novelty plants, and few bother to grow them. They believe that all bonsai should be grown outdoors in natural conditions and that there is no such thing as "indoor" bonsai.

The bonsai sold as suitable for indoors tend to be special varieties of tropical and semi-tropical trees that have been adapted for the indoor conditions in temperate countries. In their native habitat, these plants would be grown outdoors. There are also some houseplants that can be trained as bonsai. As urban space becomes more of a premium and fewer of us have the luxury of a garden, many bonsai enthusiasts have no alternative but to opt for bonsai species that are able to grow in the home, on a small balcony, or in a window box.

A camellia bonsai trained in the Informal Upright style. The tree is 3 feet (92 cm) tall and flowers profusely every year.

Why the confusion?

Why do newcomers to bonsai assume all bonsai are grown indoors? When they see bonsai for sale, they do not even bother to ask if they are for indoors or outdoors. The misconception is partly due to the popular image of bonsai promoted in movies, television advertisements, and lifestyle magazines, where dainty trees are displayed as part of the furnishings in designer homes or offices. These small and apparently delicate bonsai are created from hardy trees. They don't need protection and are capable of with-standing outdoor conditions. To add to the confusion, in the Japanese home, bonsai are often displayed in the tokonoma—a niche or alcove. Many people in the West don't realize that the bonsai are only kept in the tokonoma for a day or so before being placed back outside.

TOP RIGHT An ancient Japanese five-needle pine at a famous nursery in Nagoya, Japan. Many of the bonsai at this nursery belong to collectors who choose to keep their trees with the bonsai masters to ensure that they are cared for properly.

WHAT ARE INDOOR AND OUTDOOR BONSAI?

INDOOR BONSAI

- Indoor bonsai are not separate species. They are usually created from the particular varieties of tropical and semitropical plants that can tolerate the indoor conditions.

- Indoor bonsai are more difficult to keep because indoor conditions seldom exactly replicate the plant's natural growing environment.

- The range of reliable indoor bonsai is not as wide as the outdoor types—the most reliable indoor bonsai are created from easy-to-grow houseplants.

OUTDOOR BONSAI

- Outdoor bonsai are plants that grow naturally in the same local climatic conditions as their fully grown counterparts.

- The range of outdoor bonsai is wider because the range of plants suited to your locality will be greater than the exotic tropical and semitropical varieties available for use indoors.

- Outdoor bonsai live outdoors permanently but may be brought indoors occasionally, for up to a couple of days or so each month.

CHOOSING A PLANT

There are hundreds, if not thousands, of different varieties of plants that can be used for bonsai. Your success as a grower will depend primarily on how closely you can match the optimum growing conditions for each species. David Fukumoto of Hawaii, one of the leading indoor bonsai specialists, gives this advice: "Choose plants that will grow well in your environment, or be willing and able to modify your environment to meet the needs of the plants." If you follow this principle, you will certainly not go wrong.

 When it comes to choosing an outdoor bonsai, it makes sense to pick a variety that will thrive in your locality. If you live in a cool temperate area such as North America or Britain, you will be able to grow Japanese maples easily because their natural habitat is the cooler mountainous regions of Japan that experience similar levels of humidity, sunshine, and temperature. If you live in the tropics, cool temperate species like these will not survive; you should confine your choice to tropical varieties.

It is very disappointing when a bonsai dies, so whether indoor or outdoor, choose types of bonsai that are easy to maintain. Buy from a reputable bonsai nursery where the staff will be able to give you the best advice. A good local bonsai dealer will know how the different varieties behave and which plants are best suited to your circumstances. Choosing varieties that are easy to care for should certainly give you a head start.

Plant hardiness

The hardiness of a plant is an important consideration, especially if you live in a region that has extremely cold winters or scorching-hot summers. A plant may grow well throughout most of the year, but will die when winter comes and the temperatures plummet to below freezing or be unable to withstand a hot, dry summer. Certain plants need cold winter conditions to induce dormancy—Japanese maples and crab apples are good examples. Maples need to shed their leaves in winter and crab apples require dormancy in order to blossom in the spring. That is why these trees are therefore unsuitable for Mediterranean or tropical climates, where the winters are fairly mild. Most plants from temperate regions need freezing conditions during the winter months.

Ficus do well as outdoor bonsai in warm tropical regions. *Serissa* is also a tropical subject suitable for indoors. The Korean hornbeam is a hardy temperate tree—here you can see its fall foliage.

FICUS BENJAMINA 'NUDA'

24

WHICH PLANT?

Choose trees that are:

- easy to maintain
- hardy—winter hardy or summer hardy
- suitable for your local climate
- attractive
- personally meaningful or significant

SERISSA FOETIDA

Attractiveness

The next consideration must be the attractiveness of the plant—the color of the leaves, for example. Most people prefer bonsai with small, delicate leaves, because they create the illusion of a fully grown tree in miniature more effectively. Junipers, for instance, are very popular because their foliage is small and they are evergreen.

Significance

Some people choose varieties because they are considered lucky or because they have some special significance. In Chinese and Japanese folklore, pines and junipers are symbols of longevity—hence their popularity. The jade tree (*Crassula* species), which is also called the "money tree," is very popular with businesspeople in the Far East because it is said to bring good fortune. Certain species, such as the thorny *Euphorbia milii* (Crown of thorns), which is considered unlucky in feng shui, are avoided for superstitious reasons. Proponents of feng shui believe that bonsai should not be grown either inside or outside the house because the art represents stunted growth and is therefore unlucky. However, this doesn't seem to have deterred the great emperors and rich noblemen who kept bonsai through the ages. The choice is for each individual to make.

KOREAN HORNBEAM

25

INDOOR VARIETIES

As living spaces become more confined, the demand for indoor bonsai continues to grow. Space considerations aside, some people simply prefer their bonsai to be inside. Indoor bonsai, however, are not as easy to keep as outdoor plants and demand far more attention. Some houseplant varieties will adapt easily to life inside your home, whereas some tropical plant species require special lighting, heating, and humidification equipment. The key to success lies in choosing the right plant and becoming attuned to its individual needs.

 The range of bonsai suitable for growing indoors can be divided into three distinct groups: houseplant varieties, tropical varieties, and semitropical varieties. Each type requires different care.

Houseplant varieties

The indoor environment is an alien environment for most plants, and light levels are almost always inadequate. However, some tropical plants that can survive heavy shade, such as many species of *Ficus* and *Schefflera*, have been successfully developed for use as houseplants *(see lists on page 168)*. When these are used for indoor bonsai, they fare extremely well. They do not require special lighting or heating, which makes growing them far less complicated. The disadvantage is that the range is fairly limited and many continue to look a little like ordinary houseplants even after they have been turned into bonsai.

Tropical varieties

Many of the more exotic tropical plants, which would be grown as outdoor bonsai in their native habitats, are extremely difficult to grow as indoor bonsai in temperate countries. If you try to grow them in normal indoor conditions, without the aid of artificial lighting, heating, and humidification,

you will almost certainly be disappointed. In order to grow these plants successfully, you need to invest in specialist equipment. This can be costly to buy and operate, and you may decide it is not worth the investment.

Semitropical varieties

These bonsai include most semitropical plants and even some of our temperate and Mediterranean varieties. They, too, require slightly different care from outdoor bonsai. The most common variety on the market is the ubiquitous Chinese elm, followed by *Sageretia theezans* (Chinese bird plum cherry). Most of the plants in this group can also be grown as outdoor bonsai, provided they are given winter protection—the degree of protection will depend on where you live *(see pages 102 and 104–105)*.

SECRETS OF SUCCESS

As with outdoor bonsai, watering is the most basic requirement. How much and how often are particularly crucial to an indoor bonsai's well-being. Stand your tree on a gravel tray to make watering easier. The moisture from the tray will help to provide extra humidity for the plant.

There are many species of *Ficus* that make excellent indoor bonsai. Those that have been developed for use as houseplants are particularly good, because they can tolerate low light levels.

Temperature, light, and humidity

For tropical and semitropical plants, temperature preferences can range from 50ºF to 100ºF (10ºC–37ºC), light levels from shady to intense sunlight, and humidity from average room conditions to tropical rain forest conditions of 100 percent. With such a wide spectrum to cater for, there cannot be one single formula for success—providing the right environmental conditions means more than just adjusting the temperature. Although the average home does provide a reasonable degree of warmth, it lacks high humidity and high light levels. The amount of light you give a plant is more important than anything else, so give your bonsai as much as you can. This may be either direct sunlight or indirect light and, in some cases, high-intensity artificial light provided by fluorescent lights or metal halide lamps. A position near a window or on the windowsill itself is best.

Unfortunately, unless you go to extreme lengths and replicate tropical greenhouse conditions in the home, you have to accept that the range of plants that can be successfully grown indoors

WHY ARE INDOOR BONSAI MORE DIFFICULT TO KEEP?

Indoor bonsai are mainly tropical or semitropical trees that grow outdoors in their natural environment. When they are permanently transferred indoors in a temperate climate, they languish because the room conditions are so different. Many of the indoor varieties prefer a temperature of 60–100ºF (15–37ºC), with a humidity of 70–100 percent and bright sunshine. The average Western living room has an average temperature of 60ºF (15ºC) and only about 50 percent humidity.

will be limited to those that can tolerate slightly lower light levels, as well as lower temperature and humidity levels.

OUTDOOR VARIETIES

Climate is the biggest single factor in determining which varieties of outdoor bonsai you can grow under natural conditions in your area. Trees are highly sensitive to climatic variations. Those that grow well on one continent may not do so well in another, and regional variations exist even within a country. When considering outdoor bonsai, it makes sense to buy from a local nursery or bonsai supplier who will be knowledgeable about the plants that will thrive in your area.

 Outdoor varieties can be broadly divided into two groups: species suitable for temperate regions and those for tropical regions. Within these divisions are the subcategories of cool temperate and warm temperate, and tropical and subtropical. Mediterranean regions, however, are unique climatically because they do not fall into either of the two broad divisions. Most of the plant species covered in this book have been chosen because they grow well in temperate areas, which include North America and Britain.

Keeping outdoor bonsai

If you live by the sea or in a very windy area, a maple is not advisable because it suffers from wind scorch—pine or juniper would be a more sensible choice. Five-needle pine, beech, hornbeam, hawthorn, and crab apple also struggle in seaside areas that experience very warm, drying winds during the summer. Farther inland, these species may fare better. In some Mediterranean countries, the wide variations in air temperature and humidity make it almost impossible to grow certain varieties.

If you live in an area that enjoys a cool temperate climate, such as in Britain, Ireland, France, Holland, Belgium, southern Germany, Switzerland, northern Italy, the northeastern United States and Canada, you will be able to grow most of the varieties that are commonly grown in central Japan. If you live in an area that has extremes of temperature, such as the midwestern United States and Canada, and northern Europe, you will be able to grow the usual temperate plants, but they will need to be protected in winter *(see pages 104–105)*. Whatever your local climate, you will still have a wide range of species from which to choose—whether as part of a normal garden, or as ornamentation in a dry-landscape, or Zen, garden.

WHY ARE OUTDOOR BONSAI EASIER TO KEEP?

Outdoor bonsai are created from species that are suited to the local climate. These plants will thrive because they do not have to struggle against the elements. Plants that are grown outdoors benefit from sunshine, fresh air, and rain. The only unnatural aspect of their state is that they are constrained by a container. However, provided you water an outdoor bonsai regularly and feed it from time to time, there is no reason why it should not survive for many years.

CLOCKWISE FROM LEFT
An ancient Chinese "Itoi-gawa" juniper with natural driftwood; one of the many Japanese maples suitable for deciduous bonsai; a Zen garden.

Each species has its own particular charm. In Japan and Europe, Chinese juniper and Japanese yew have become very desirable because they lend themselves easily to driftwood effects on the trunk and branches. Driftwood effects are created by carving dead wood to mimic the appearance of silvery, bleached branches that are the result of weathering and storm damage—currently very fashionable in the bonsai world *(see page 47)*. The many different varieties of Chinese juniper include the hugely popular "Itoi-gawa" and "Kisu" as well as "Sonare," "Hotoku," and "Kaizuka." Other evergreens such as the needle juniper, black pine, white pine, and *Cryptomeria* are also popular and not as expensive *(see* Plant Directory, *pages 166–167)*.

If you have a green thumb and can grow plants successfully in controlled environments such as heated greenhouses and cool shade houses, the range of varieties that you can grow as bonsai can be increased considerably. Many semitropical trees that are normally sold as indoor bonsai in temperate countries will grow better as outdoor subjects in the summer with slight protection in winter.

SECRETS OF SUCCESS

Always choose species that are known to thrive in the local climate. Don't experiment: If a plant struggles to survive, it will eventually die. Pines and maples will not grow in the Middle East, so there is no point even trying. People who live in hot countries sometimes try growing trees from temperate climates in spaces that are air-conditioned, but they are seldom successful.

3

BUYING
AND PRICING
BONSAI

*"The value of a bonsai cannot always
be measured in terms of money."*

WHERE TO BUY

When it comes to buying bonsai, you can spend as little or as much as you choose. At one end of the spectrum, there are cheap and cheerful starter plants; at the other, exquisite specimens created by bonsai masters that collectors buy as investments. Whatever your budget, take time researching the options and think about what kind of plant would best suit your situation. Most people like to acquire the finished article. Growing a bonsai from seed *(see pages 74–75)* or waiting years for a tree to mature are options only if you want them to be.

Before you buy, find out as much as possible about what's available. The Internet is a good starting point, provided you select some trustworthy sources. Double-check your information by consulting respected organizations such as botanical gardens, bonsai associations, and horticultural societies. Your nearest bonsai nursery should also be able to give you sound, unbiased advice. You can buy bonsai from a wide variety of outlets, including garden centers, department stores, and florists. However, a specialist supplier can offer far more choice, and the sales staff is more likely to be able to give you expert advice.

Bonsai nurseries

The best place to buy bonsai is from your nearest reputable bonsai nursery. Check out the nursery beforehand by consulting your local or national horticultural or bonsai society. The main advantage of these centers, where the bonsai are looked after by specialists, is that you can view the plants in their optimum growing environment and learn about their likes and dislikes from the outset. A specialized outlet will also stock all the necessary tools, fertilizers, wire, pots, and manuals. Because the other customers are likely to be bonsai enthusiasts, you can often pick up useful tips and information from them, too.

Garden and plant centers

As the popularity of bonsai has grown, many garden and plant centers have begun to stock them. They generally have the common indoor varieties, such as Chinese elm, *Serissa*, and *Sagaretia*, and some also offer a range of outdoor varieties, such as Japanese maple, pine, and juniper. The choice may not be as wide as at a specialist bonsai nursery, but the plants are usually well maintained.

In tropical and Mediterranean countries, bougainvillea varieties make exquisite bonsai. They flower profusely and over a very long period. In temperate regions, they are grown as indoor bonsai.

Should anything go wrong, such as the tree suddenly losing all its leaves, you have the comfort of knowing that a reputable garden center will replace the plant or give you a refund. Nothing could be more disheartening than meeting with failure with your very first bonsai.

Florists

Flower shops usually sell houseplants and occasionally a few bonsai. Most florists maintain a fairly humid atmosphere in their stores, and indoor bonsai will keep well in these conditions. Outdoor bonsai, however, will tolerate such an atmosphere only for a couple of weeks and, if kept in a store for longer periods, will develop long straggly shoots. An outdoor bonsai kept indoors will grow as if it is summer, which means it will have a problem adjusting to the natural climate once you take it home and place it outdoors. The staff at a florist's may not necessarily know the difference between an indoor bonsai and an outdoor one, so consider any purchase carefully.

The author's nursery, where thousands of imported and homegrown bonsai can be seen. A visit to a bonsai nursery can give you lots of ideas on how to grow and display your trees.

Department and hardware stores

Unless you are buying from a department store in Japan, where bonsai are displayed on the rooftop garden, buying from a department or hardware store is not recommended, because the bonsai are almost always displayed in an inappropriate environment. Their position is usually too warm, too dark, and too dry. Indoor bonsai may survive in these conditions for a few days, but outdoor bonsai cannot.

SECRETS OF SUCCESS

Like any work of art, a bonsai is best viewed firsthand. If a trip to a specialist bonsai nursery is out of the question, buying mail-order from a reputable bonsai supplier is the next best option.

IMPORTING BONSAI

The bonsai market is heavily restricted by horticultural import regulations. The plant varieties that are permitted into each country vary considerably. In the United States, the authorities permit the entry of pines and junipers but not deciduous trees such as maples. In Canada, maples are allowed entry but not pines and junipers. Some plant species are subject to the CITES convention (Convention on International Trade in Endangered Species of Wild Flora and Fauna).

Q **Can I bring a bonsai home with me from abroad?**

A It's not advisable unless you have checked your facts carefully and are absolutely sure importation is legal. Consult your government agricultural department or ministry and follow the regulations and procedures to the letter. The consequences of flouting the law could be very serious for the indigenous flora of your home country. Some countries insist on a quarantine period of several months to ensure that imported plants are completely free of organisms that could endanger indigenous plant species.

Q **What's the best way to buy an imported bonsai?**

A The best place to buy bonsai is always a specialist nursery in your own country.

Q **What about buying over the Internet?**

A Approach with caution. It is not advisable to buy from a foreign supplier based outside your country's jurisdiction. If you live in the U.S., don't buy from Europe or Asia without prior permission from the Department of Agriculture. Unfortunately, many Internet dealers are small-time operators. Even if well intentioned, they may not be familiar with the regulations governing the export of plants. If a bonsai is shipped without adequate documentation, it may be impounded by customs.

SHOPPING FOR A BONSAI

Questions to ask when buying a bonsai:

- Is it an indoor or outdoor variety?
- How long has it been at the store or nursery?
- When was it last repotted? Ask if it is possible to see the root ball.
- When does it need repotting again?
- When was it last fed and when will it need feeding again?
- What is the best fertilizer to use? How much and how often?
- When was it last trimmed and when will it need trimming again?

- From which pests and diseases does this species typically suffer?
- What is the tree's approximate age?
- From where did it originate?
- Does the store or nursery offer a holiday-care service for bonsai?
- What is the best way to care for this tree? You can judge how knowledgeable staff members are by their answers. Their general attitude and helpfulness will also give you a good indication of the quality of the nursery or store.

If you travel to China, this is what you will often come across at a bonsai market. Don't be tempted to buy bonsai to bring back home from abroad—customs authorities will impound them.

Club events and conventions

Bonsai club events and conventions have become very popular among bonsai enthusiasts. Many dealers and nurseries attend these events to sell bonsai and accessories. The selection of plants is usually excellent, and prices are very competitive. The only disadvantage is that the dealer is unlikely to be based in your local area, which makes it difficult to return a plant should any problems arise.

Mail-order and Internet shopping

Providing the supplier is reputable, buying bonsai by mail order can be extremely convenient. Many bonsai specialists operate a mail-order service, selling tools and supplies as well as plants, in addition to their nursery outlet. The biggest dis-advantage of buying this way is that you cannot be completely sure of what you are getting. Be wary if a bonsai is being offered at a rock-bottom price. The chances are that it's just a seedling or young plant, with no training at all. You should also check the delivery options. A tree will suffer if it spends more than four or five days in transit or during hot weather, more than three or four days.

Buying on an Internet auction site may land you a bargain, but your purchase may come without any guarantee. In some cases, the bonsai being offered for sale has later been identified as stolen.

Sales and auctions

Very occasionally, a bonsai collection is put up for sale by one of the large auction houses. These events are usually well attended by collectors and can be a good source of quality trees. However, there's no hope of a refund should you discover a tree has problems once you've bought it. For this reason, it pays to get someone who is knowledgeable about bonsai to give you advice on quality and value when you view. You may even consider getting an agent to bid on your behalf.

Private individuals and growers

Many bonsai growers sell trees privately, either over the Internet or through newspaper advertisements. The quality varies, and unless you are sure of what you are buying, it is best not to risk such a purchase. When you buy from an individual, rather than a registered business, you have no recourse for complaint if you discover a problem with your tree once you have handed over your money.

SECRETS OF SUCCESS

Ask the mail-order supplier or Internet seller to send you a picture of the bonsai you are interested in before you commit.

FINDING A BARGAIN

Bonsai can take years to create, so they tend to be more expensive than ordinary plants. You are also paying for the pot, which may add considerably to the overall price, along with country of origin and importation costs. All these factors mean bargains are hard to find. If a bonsai is being offered at a discount, it usually has something wrong with it—it might be misshapen or have lost a branch or two. Some nurseries have genuine sales to move stock that they want to clear, but you should always check that the trees are in good condition.

You can normally tell whether a tree is healthy quite easily, especially in spring and summer when it is in full growth. If you are buying at this time of year, check that the tree's foliage is fresh and green and that there is lots of new growth.

In autumn and winter, when deciduous foliage is about to turn yellow and even the evergreens are beginning to look tired, signs of health or other problems are difficult to detect. If you have any doubts, ask to see the root ball. If the bonsai dealer or grower has confidence in the tree, he or she should have no qualms about showing you the condition of a tree's roots. The only time that this may not be possible is if the tree has been recently repotted.

When the root ball is removed from its pot, smell the soil to check that it is not putrid. Healthy trees have healthy roots, which usually smell like fresh mushrooms. If the root ball appears waterlogged, the tree is suffering from poor drainage. If you have the expertise to remedy the problem, insist that the price reflect the poor condition of the tree or preferably choose a healthier specimen. Some growers may not like your bargaining in this way, but it is always worth a try. Be sure to ask when the tree was last repotted. If the dealer does not know, ask when it should next be repotted. Don't be shy about asking these questions. A responsible dealer will want to share information about his or her stock and will be happy to give you advice on how to care for your bonsai so that you can enjoy it for as long as possible.

It is also important to check that the pot is in good condition. A ceramic pot should not be cracked or broken and if it is, the price should reflect this.

A bonsai in a plastic pot should also be less expensive. If you do not like the pot the tree is in, or if the pot is particularly expensive, try offering to buy the tree without its pot—this may help to bring the price down a bit.

A Hinoki cypress bonsai. Good specimens are fairly expensive and keeping them in top condition requires meticulous attention.

SECRETS OF SUCCESS

If you are buying several bonsai or one very expensive specimen, try negotiating to reduce the price or see if you can get a few extras thrown in "for free." The nursery will want to keep you as a long-term customer, and if you show loyalty, you stand a better chance of preferential treatment. Pick your moment: buying during the off-season, which usually means winter, will give you more scope for bargaining.

BUYING CHECKLIST

Decide on indoor or outdoor bonsai.

If indoor, choose from the following:

- an ordinary houseplant bonsai
- a tropical species that requires supplementary lighting and heating
- a semitropical bonsai that can be put outdoors in the summer

If outdoor, choose from the following:

- evergreen
- deciduous
- flowering

Consider style: Single, Double or Multitrunk; Informal upright, Formal upright, Slanting, Cascade, Windswept *(see chapter 4)*.

Consider size: Bonsai can range from a couple of inches (6 cm) to 3 or 4 feet (1 m). Decide where your plant will be positioned and how you want the space to be filled.

Consider price: How much do you want to spend, and on how many plants?

A red 'Deshojo' maple in the author's collection. It is a Raft planting—i.e., a single tree connected by a common sinuous root. This is a large specimen, 41 inches (102 cm) high and 43 inches (108 cm) wide. It is a majestic-looking composition. It is a high-value specimen because it is beautiful, rare, and the style is very unusual.

PRICING AND VALUES

Bonsai are relatively expensive items, and it's not difficult to see why. Ordinary bedding and herbaceous plants take just a couple of months to produce—and even large trees take no more than six or seven years—whereas a bonsai may take decades. Like wine, a good bonsai cannot be hurried. There are many reasons why certain bonsai are more expensive than others, although age is an important factor in determining quality and value. The older a bonsai, the more valuable it is likely to be.

As a work of art, with no practical use, the worth of a bonsai depends on the buyer's perspective. A precious specimen may be worth a great deal to a keen collector or nothing at all to someone with no appreciation of the artistry involved. Its value as a commodity derives from the fact that it can be traded in the marketplace, and the amount buyers are prepared to pay for it.

In today's global market, the prices and values of goods and services are determined by supply and demand, not just within individual countries, but all around the world. To supply bonsai takes considerable time and skill, which in itself limits supply. The fact that there are only two major producers of bonsai—China and Japan—also has a limiting effect. The restrictions governing the export trade add a third impediment to free supply. Bonsai that are easy to produce and obtain are relatively cheap because the supply is plentiful, but good-quality specimens are becoming increasingly rare and consequently more expensive.

Importation costs

A bonsai bought in Japan may sell for three or four times the price in Europe or the United States. Currency fluctuations aside, the increase reflects the cost and administration of importation. First, there are the export and import formalities, such as the licenses. The importer also has to comply with phyto-sanitary (plant health) requirements.

Bonsai for export are transported by air or by sea. Packing is a skilled job, and great care has to be taken to ensure the bonsai is not damaged in any way. If the specimen is an expensive one, breaking so much as a branch can substantially lower its value. Bonsai that are transported by sea

Bougainvillea grown in the Semi-cascade style.

A bonsai exhibit at the Chelsea Flower Show, London, England. These trees belong to amateur enthusiasts who spend years perfecting each individual tree. They may have a price tag, but it would be impossible to put a value on these trees because they are almost like children to those who own them.

are carried in refrigerated containers, and their temperature is carefully monitored. When they arrive in the importing country, government officials have to make their own inspection to satisfy themselves that the plants are free from harmful organisms. Many imported plants have to be quarantined. The length of quarantine can vary from a couple of months to a couple of years, depending on the country. A bonsai cannot be sold during this time, which adds more to the eventual price tag.

Not all bonsai survive the rigors of fumigation and chemical treatment, and a certain percentage dies on arrival. Allowing for this constitutes another cost to be added to the import duty and other tariffs levied by the customs authorities on arrival.

Finally, you have to factor in the overhead costs, such as rent, rates, wages, and advertising, that the importer has to recover, the profit margin that keeps the business viable, and the taxes levied on the dealer when he takes his share of the profit.

By the time you buy your bonsai from your local nursery, it will probably have changed hands many times. A succession of dealers and growers will buy and sell a bonsai—each time adding a little more value and quality to the tree as it moves up the chain. A really old and fine specimen bonsai will have changed ownership countless times over the years.

However, it does not necessarily follow that a tree increases in value each time it changes hands. It may lose value if it has been neglected. On the other hand, a tree that has been worked on by a famous master will appreciate considerably. The master's touch may alter the tree so that it bears no resemblance to its former self. Bonsai dealers in Japan attend auctions for trees just as car dealers attend car auctions, with the sole purpose of making a profit.

Why is there a demand for bonsai? For an enthusiast, it is not so much the price of the tree that matters, but what a bonsai can do for you. An exquisite bonsai has the capacity to speak to one's innermost self. And that kind of quality cannot be measured solely in monetary terms.

BONSAI AS INVESTMENTS

A good-quality tree that is properly looked after can be a sound investment. However, you should fully understand the bonsai scene before you consider speculating in this way. Predicting how trends and fashions in bonsai will develop is the key to making the right purchase, and as with any other investment, there is a risk involved.

PRICE FACTORS

There are a number of factors that determine the value and, therefore, the price, of a bonsai. Each factor has a bearing, and some are more important than others. But the key determinant is beauty. How this is assessed can be highly subjective, but fortunately a beautiful bonsai is not difficult to spot. It has that special quality we call charisma. Charismatic bonsai are like charismatic people—they stand out in a crowd!

INDOOR OR OUTDOOR

Indoor bonsai are usually less expensive than outdoor bonsai for several reasons. The quality of indoor bonsai is generally not as high as that of outdoor varieties and this is reflected in the price. Also, indoor bonsai tend to be less expensive to produce. They are typically tropical or semitropical and come from China or Korea, where production costs are low. Outdoor bonsai, which are temperate species, are mainly imported from Japan, where costs are much higher. Speed of production is another factor. Tropical trees grow at a much faster rate: the lead times are probably half that of temperate outdoor trees.

FICUS

SIZE

Large bonsai are usually more impressive than small bonsai, and as a rule, price increases with size, but a small bonsai may be more expensive than a much larger tree if the quality is superior. Although size is not everything, it does matter in bonsai. Larger trees take longer to grow and are more difficult to make into bonsai, so this adds to the cost. Larger trees also require much larger pots, and these are more expensive to buy than small ones. Larger-size trees involve greater handling and shipping costs.

This large trident maple has been in the author's collection for the past 12 years and is nearly 90 years old. It took three generations of Japanese growers to produce it. It is 47 inches (118 cm) wide and 38 inches (96 cm) high and has a root spread of 16 inches (40 cm). Its high quality and impressive size make it extremely valuable.

TRIDENT MAPLE

SPECIES

Certain species are considered more desirable than others, although what is popular in one country may not be popular in another. In the East, pines and junipers are considered lucky because they are symbols of longevity, so they are always popular. On the other hand, thorny plants are unpopular because they are said to bring bad luck or bad feng shui. In Mediterranean countries, maples and many temperate-flowering subjects such as crab apple, which require dormancy in winter and struggle to survive are there-fore less popular. Chinese junipers have in recent years become very fashionable both in Japan and in Europe, especially if they have nice driftwood effects *(see below)* on the trunks. They are highly sought after by collectors and consequently are very expensive.

CHINESE JUNIPER

DRIFTWOOD

STYLE

Driftwood *(see page 47)* and twisted trunks have always been fashion-able, and in the last two decades they have become even more popular, due largely to the pioneering work of that great bonsai master and sculptor Masahiko Kimura. Any evergreen bonsai that has driftwood will be expen-sive. Some styles that are difficult to create, such as the Root over rock and Broom styles *(see page 55)*, also fetch higher prices because of the complexity and long lead times involved in making them. Some styles cease to be fashionable because tastes change. The Exposed root *(see page 55)* and other highly contorted styles are good examples.

POT OR CONTAINER

The pot in which the plant grows also has a bearing on its value. An antique Chinese pot, particularly if it is very old—i.e., over 100 years old—could be worth more than the tree. The Chinese have been making bonsai pots for well over a 1,000 years and the Japanese for the last 400 or 500 years. Antique pots from Yixing in China and those from the Tokoname, Bizen, Seto, and the Shigaraki area of Japan, are particularly valuable. Experts can recognize them even without looking at their seals, which are usually stamped on the bottom of each pot. Contemporary pots made by famous potters and from the well-known kilns in Japan also command high prices. Look for well-made pots and pots that have a patina or look old.

HANDMADE POTS

AGE

Most people associate bonsai with age, and the older the tree the more valuable it is likely to be. When buying a bonsai, never accept the stated age of the tree as gospel. Most ages are only an estimate. You should leave a good margin for error. A genuinely old tree is valuable, but it should not be the sole factor that determines its value *(see pages 58–59 on size and age)*. The age of a bonsai is sometimes counted by the number of generations that it has taken to develop the tree. If a generation is roughly 30 years, then a 100-year-old tree will be described as a three- or four-generation tree.

TRIDENT MAPLE

JAPANESE WHITE PINE

PROVENANCE

Has the tree got a pedigree and history? Has it been worked on by a famous master and maintained by a famous nursery? Bonsai that win prizes at major bonsai exhibitions, such as the Kokofu-ten and Sakafu-ten, which are held annually in Japan, become famous icons of the bonsai world *(see box below)*. The entry procedure for these competitions is so tough that simply being selected adds to a bonsai's value. As interest in bonsai spreads, we may begin to see the same phenomenon in the West. Trees that have been made or owned by famous bonsai masters in the West, such as the late John Naka, will no doubt be highly collectable.

FAMOUS BONSAI

In Japan, famous bonsai are like pop idols or film stars. Their reputation goes before them. They are known by names such as "Dragon Flying into Clouds" or "Whispering Giant" and appear in books and magazines, where they are immediately recognized. These bonsai stars acquire their notoriety from winning prizes at major bonsai exhibitions.

FAKES

In bonsai, age can be faked to a degree, but the attempt is easily detected. Old pots are difficult to fake, but have a rather limited following in the West because not many bonsai enthusiasts are ceramics experts. Most people buy pots just because they like them. Driftwood in certain bonsai, especially junipers, can be faked, but an experienced bonsai grower will notice.

MARKET TRENDS

Fashion in bonsai plays a major role in determining popularity and therefore price. You only have to look at the bonsai manuals of the 1960s to see how radically tastes have moved on. Fashion has affected the pots as well as the growing and creative techniques. Today evergreens, in particular the Chinese juniper, take center stage. Trees that include a lot of driftwood *(see pages 47, 130–133)* are also popular. Shapes and styles are continually evolving. In Japan, collecting bonsai is now essentially a hobby for the older generation, but in the West, most collectors and enthusiasts are younger people.

1960s JUNIPER

CONDITION

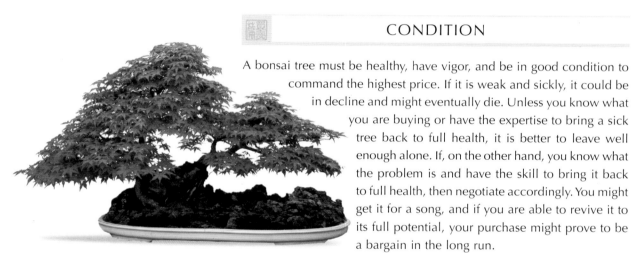

RED 'DESHOJO' MAPLE

A bonsai tree must be healthy, have vigor, and be in good condition to command the highest price. If it is weak and sickly, it could be in decline and might eventually die. Unless you know what you are buying or have the expertise to bring a sick tree back to full health, it is better to leave well enough alone. If, on the other hand, you know what the problem is and have the skill to bring it back to full health, then negotiate accordingly. You might get it for a song, and if you are able to revive it to its full potential, your purchase might prove to be a bargain in the long run.

QUALITY OF SPECIFIC PARTS

Buyers will study specific aspects of a tree, such as the roots, trunk, branches, apex, and so on. Seldom will you find a tree that is perfect in every respect. If you do, the tree will be very valuable indeed and will be priced accordingly. It is more usual to find a tree with one or two good features, such as a good root spread, or "nebari" *(see page 51),* as it is called in Japanese, or good branches and a poor trunk or apex. If a tree has one or two faults that can be corrected by reshaping over a period of time, then it might be worth buying as a long-term project. It might even prove to be a good investment.

GOOD NEBARI

4

BONSAI AESTHETICS

"A bonsai can inspire and elevate the human spirit."

WHAT MAKES A GOOD BONSAI?

Bonsai come in many different shapes, sizes, styles, and species. Even within the same species, you will come across different styles. The choice can be bewildering. It can be difficult to know what to look for—should you consider first the color, the shape, the interesting trunk, or the overall appearance? What exactly is it that makes a bonsai specimen "good"?

 Whenever you visit a bonsai nursery, the first thing to note is the general health of the trees. If they are lush and growing vigorously, you can buy with confidence. Never buy a tree that looks sick, even if it seems like a bargain. Choice is also important: the more, the better. If the grower has only a few items displayed, you are less likely to find a tree that is right for you.

Because the objective of a bonsai—the plant and its pot combined—is to be beautiful, judging the extent to which this has been achieved will ultimately always be a matter of opinion. But even in the realm of aesthetics, rules can be applied. In bonsai, beauty is traditionally assessed in terms of nature. Bonsai are trees, after all. Bonsai artists create various shapes and styles, but the most successful are those that look the most natural. There can be no doubt that nature has an intrinsic beauty—who would refute the beauty of a snowflake pattern, the structure of leaves and flowers, or of rock strata? The beauty of nature is the standard by which humans judge everything else. A bonsai that bears no resemblance to its form in the wild will therefore not be convincing. Even if it is nature at its most extreme, it is the source from which all great bonsai artists draw inspiration. The artist is presenting a scaled-down impression of what he or she sees growing in the natural world.

SECRETS OF SUCCESS

All bonsai artists should strive for naturalness in their creations. The two fundamental principles of Zen aesthetics, wabi and sabi *(see pages 112–113)* are based on the key concepts of simplicity, tranquillity, and naturalness. A good bonsai should possess all these qualities, but naturalness is perhaps the most important.

DRIFTWOOD EFFECTS

Driftwood effects are found in nature on trees that grow under very harsh conditions, such as in deserts or in the high mountains. When parts of a tree die, the wind, sun, snow, and rain erode the dead wood, creating exquisite, natural sculpture. Driftwood effects—either on the branches, termed "jin," or on the main trunk itself, "shari"—are currently very fashionable and have come to play a major role in contemporary bonsai *(see pages 130–133)*. Although driftwood is not new in the bonsai world, it has become an extremely popular feature over the last 25 years, due largely to the innovative work of the great Japanese master Masahiko Kimura. Gifted bonsai artists are able to carve the dead wood with great skill to produce stunning results. Driftwood effects are best on evergreen coniferous species, although some tropical varieties, such as *Pemphis*, look striking with driftwood, too.

PEMPHIS ACIDULA

Some of the finest bonsai in the world are kept at this nursery in Nagoya, Japan. Everything here is of the highest quality and is in good health.

WHAT TO LOOK FOR

The first impression you have of a bonsai is of its overall appearance. This will include the shape of the tree, the general directional movement, and any outstanding feature. You can then very quickly assess general health, vigor, and age. Finally, you should scrutinize the tree's roots, trunk, branches, and pot—in that order. Here is a brief overview of what to look for when you view a bonsai.

SHAPE AND CHARACTER

CHINESE JUNIPER

A bonsai with good overall shape is like a person who has an attractive face, is well proportioned, and has good posture. A tree that has all these qualities is highly prized. Sometimes a bonsai may have a natural treelike form or a unique feature that makes it special—an interesting trunk or some dramatic driftwood effect, for example. The unique quality of a bonsai is sometimes the result of an accident of nature, which manifests itself as an exquisite imperfection. When a characteristic of this kind is combined with an antique element and a natural primitive look, an ordinary tree is transformed into something extraordinary. This juniper is of average height, with a well-balanced overall shape, an attractive trunk with just a hint of driftwood, and is in superb condition. The strong-looking rectangular pot with slightly round edges is also appropriate for the character of this tree.

MOUNTAIN MAPLE

STYLE

Style is a convenient way of describing a particular genre of bonsai. For instance, we could refer to a bonsai as a "Twin-trunk tree grown in the Japanese style" or a "Literati-style tree grown in the Chinese style," and so on. It is not something one would especially look for unless you are looking for a particular style of bonsai to complement your collection. Style is of little consequence in its own right. It isn't something that adds or detracts from a tree's beauty. Some of the world's finest bonsai do not conform to any of the recognized styles, and yet they are stunning. Bonsai buffs derive immense satisfaction from knowing the names of all the different styles, since this gives them a sense of one-upmanship. (Style is covered more fully on *pages 52–57*.)

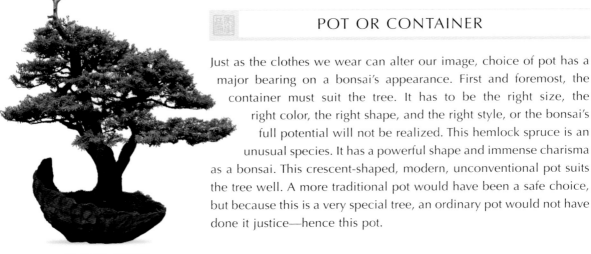

POT OR CONTAINER

Just as the clothes we wear can alter our image, choice of pot has a major bearing on a bonsai's appearance. First and foremost, the container must suit the tree. It has to be the right size, the right color, the right shape, and the right style, or the bonsai's full potential will not be realized. This hemlock spruce is an unusual species. It has a powerful shape and immense charisma as a bonsai. This crescent-shaped, modern, unconventional pot suits the tree well. A more traditional pot would have been a safe choice, but because this is a very special tree, an ordinary pot would not have done it justice—hence this pot.

HEMLOCK SPRUCE

SIZE AND AGE

CHINESE JUNIPER

Although bonsai has always been associated with great age, it is not the most important criterion in determining quality. A bonsai can be very old, but if it is not beautiful, its age counts for little. These two examples are both junipers. The juniper pictured below is well over 200 years old, and the Chinese Juniper on the right is just 10 years old. Both are exquisite in their own way.

The size of a bonsai provokes different emotions. A large tree gives a feeling of grandeur and majesty, while a small bonsai imparts a special Alice-in-Wonderland charm. Ultimately, it comes down to personal preference or necessity. In Japan, for example, small bonsai are popular because most people live in small apartments. If you have a large garden, then the size of bonsai does not really matter. In Hong Kong, however, where high-rise living is the rule rather than the exception, bonsai enthusiasts grow very large bonsai—some of the trees are in excess of 6 feet (2 m). They get around the problem of space by growing their trees in gardens that are owned by a bonsai society.

ANCIENT JUNIPER ORIGINALLY COLLECTED FROM THE MOUNTAINS

COLOR

Deciduous trees change color with the seasons: in the spring the new leaves emerge as green, bronze, or red, and in the fall they present a kaleidoscope of colors ranging from pale gold to fiery crimson. Flowers and fruit also offer a rich palette of color *(see pages 64–65)*. Color reminds us of the changing seasons; it brings us out of hibernation in the spring and soothes our tired minds when the autumn leaves begin to fall. Even evergreens have their distinctive shades of green. Color certainly enriches our enjoyment of bonsai. Our trees would not be the same without it.

JAPANESE 'DISSECTUM' MAPLE

TRIDENT MAPLE

THE TRUNK

The trunk's aesthetic function is probably the most important—the trunk is what gives a bonsai its classification by style *(see pages 54–57)*. As the trunk emerges from the soil surface, its base should appear to rise from the roots with immense power. The trunk base is considered so important that the Japanese refer to it using a special term—"tachi-agari." The upper portion of the trunk should taper off gradually to a narrower point. Trees that have a "chopped" appearance toward the apex, or end abruptly, are considered defective.

THE BRANCHES

Branches give the bonsai its silhouette and shape. They also provide the finer detail, which can make the difference between a good bonsai and an exquisite specimen. They help to convey the mood or feeling of the tree simply by the way they are pruned, arranged, and shaped. Thick, heavy, or mature branches give the feeling of great age, as do branches that hang downward—all of these are particularly important qualities in conifers. Light, delicate, and airy branches suggest femininity, as do upward-growing branches, all of which are characteristic of Japanese maples. Bonsai that have been trained for a long time usually have a great many finely developed branches and twigs. This effect is known as "ramification" and in deciduous species, is best appreciated in winter when the tree is without its leaves. Good ramification is one of the hallmarks of a fine-specimen bonsai.

JAPANESE HORNBEAM

50

MAPLE ROOTS

ROOTS

Aside from the tree's overall appearance and center of attraction, the visible surface roots—not the roots inside the pot—are a bonsai's most important feature. The Japanese refer to these surface roots as the "nebari." A good show of roots gives the tree the impression of stability and permanence and makes a bonsai look imperious and powerful. A bonsai that does not possess good surface roots resembles a telegraph pole that has been stuck into the ground. Older trees tend to have a good buttress, which gives the impression that the tree is firmly anchored. A fine-specimen bonsai should always have beautiful surface roots.

HEALTH AND VIGOR

If a bonsai is not looked after properly, it will not live very long. A healthy tree looks vibrant and strong, while a sick tree lacks luster and appears limp. Aside from watering, bonsai need to be fed, repotted, and trimmed on a regular basis. If you are not able to keep your bonsai healthy, seek help from someone who has the expertise. Bonsai clubs and nurseries can usually help. In Japan, there is a long tradition of nurseries taking care of famous trees. In fact, many bonsai masters earn their living doing this, seeing to the regular maintenance and preparing the trees for the famous exhibitions. In the West, discriminating collectors of bonsai are now following this tradition, having realized that owning good bonsai involves more than simply keeping them watered. Maintenance involves grooming and rewiring on a regular basis.

OLD CHINESE JUNIPER

JAPANESE WISTERIA

FLOWERS AND FRUIT

Some bonsai are grown especially for their flowers and fruit. Satsuki azaleas, apricot, crab apple, and wisteria are good examples. The other aspects such as the trunk, branches, and roots, although important, are not as highly regarded as the flowers or fruit for which the bonsai are mainly grown. This is not to say that other factors are neglected—they are in fact seen for the greater part of the year when the flowers and fruit are not around. So, they also need to be in excellent condition. The example pictured is Japanese wisteria (*Wisteria floribunda* 'Violacea plena').

STYLE AND ETHNICITY

In bonsai, the term "style" can be used to refer to one of two things. It can either describe the tree's ethnic style, most commonly Chinese- or Japanese-style bonsai, or it can be applied to a tree's physical attributes, such as single trunk, double trunk, slanting, or cascade. People who have been brought up in the tradition of Japanese bonsai normally associate the term "style" with the latter point. Style is therefore just another word for genre. It is a convenient way of describing a particular type of bonsai.

 The bonsai tradition has its earliest roots in China, where it was first practiced some two millennia ago. The Japanese interest dates back to around 1100 CE, when Buddhist priests took the art from China to Japan. For centuries, the Japanese simply copied Chinese-style bonsai. It wasn't until the early 20th century that a distinct Japanese style of bonsai emerged.

In the last 30 or 40 years, the rest of the world has also developed an interest in bonsai and there is now a following on every continent and in every country. Each country's culture has inevitably influenced the aesthetic interpretation of bonsai. Consequently, there has now emerged a "European style," an "American style," an "Indonesian style," and so on.

Commercially, the Chinese and Japanese styles still dominate. Chinese style tends to be restricted to indoor tropical varieties, while Japanese style is represented by the hardy outdoor bonsai sold in nurseries across Europe and North America. Each style encompasses significant differences and regional variations, but generally speaking, the Chinese style tends to be more ornate and ornamental, whereas the Japanese style is simpler and follows clean lines. Both generic styles are popular.

Bonsai enthusiasts would describe this tree as a Japanese bonsai in the Slanting style.

STYLE Q & A

Q Is one generic style superior to another?

A No, because you are not comparing like with like. Popularity tends to be determined by cultural conditioning: in China, for example, the Japanese style is not so popular and vice versa. Your choice will be limited by what your local bonsai nursery has to offer.

Q Are some shapes superior to others?

A No style is intrinsically better. Some styles, such as Literati (Bunjin) are enjoying more popularity because in today's climate they are considered to reflect good taste. Driftwood style is also very much in vogue.

Q Are some shape styles rarer than others?

A You don't see many Root-over-rock, Raft, or Cascade styles because they are particularly difficult to create. Therefore, good examples of these tend to draw more attention and command a higher price.

Q How can I be sure my bonsai is authentic?

A When a generic style is imitated out of context—in another country, for example—it invariably carries the stamp of the local artist. This is how new generic styles evolve. The variation of styles is part of what makes the bonsai scene so rich.

Shape styles

Within each generic, or ethnic, style are three broad categories and a dozen or more subcategories of bonsai shapes, which are also referred to as "styles." The classifications, which may seem confusing at first, are only a means to an end. If you can refer to a bonsai by style (see Choosing a Style on pages 54–57), other enthusiasts will be able to picture it more easily. Thus, a bonsai with a straight, perpendicular trunk is called a "Formal upright," whereas one that has a slanting trunk is a bonsai in the "Slanting style," and so on. Styles are therefore a convenient way of describing the various shapes in bonsai.

Sometimes a bonsai may not fall into any particular style, but this does not invalidate it as a bonsai. Such a bonsai is very likely to stand out on account of its uniqueness.

The bonsai in this garden are all in the Chinese style. The large tree is a Twin-trunk bonsai. The setting is The Chinese Garden at the Montreal Botanic Gardens, Canada.

CHOOSING A STYLE

The different shapes in bonsai that are generally referred to as styles can be grouped into three broad categories according to the number of trunks: single-trunk styles; multiple-trunk styles; and multiple-tree, group or forest styles. The names given to these styles serve as a universal datum or reference point for all bonsai enthusiasts throughout the world.

SINGLE-TRUNK STYLES

FORMAL UPRIGHT

INFORMAL UPRIGHT

SLANTING

WINDSWEPT

CASCADE

SEMI-CASCADE

LITERATI (BUNJIN)

BROOM

WEEPING

PLANTED ON ROCK

ROOT OVER ROCK

SPLIT TRUNK

DRIFTWOOD

COILED

EXPOSED ROOT

MULTIPLE-TRUNK STYLES

TWIN TRUNK

TRIPLE TRUNK

MULTIPLE TRUNK

ROOT CONNECTED MULTIPLE TRUNK, OR RAFT

MULTIPLE-TREE, GROUP, OR FOREST STYLE

FOREST OR GROUP PLANTING

FOREST OR GROUP PLANTED ON ROCK

LANDSCAPE

This large *Celtis sinensis* is grown in a rather unconventional Twin-trunk style.

SIZE AND AGE

Size and age usually go hand-in-hand in bonsai, but not without exception. A large tree may be relatively young if it has been grown fast. And a bonsai that appears old may turn out to be a fake. Most people associate bonsai with age. The stereotypical image of a bonsai is gnarled and twisted. An ancient tree has a mystique that younger trees do not possess. Indeed, one of the original objectives of the Taoist priests who experimented with bonsai more than a thousand years ago was to slow the sap rising in a tree to prolong its life.

Age

Bonsai are still revered for their antiquity, especially in China and Japan, as well as in Korea and Taiwan, where the art is also practiced. The age of a bonsai seems to capture the public's imagination and engender a particular fascination. At exhibitions, for example, "How old is that tree?" is one of the most frequently asked questions. Age is paramount as far as these people are concerned, and the beauty and rarity of species are only secondary considerations to them.

The author with a massive five-needle pine bonsai in the Shanghai Botanic Garden in China. This tree has been in training for over a century.

The influence of the West

Over the last 20 or 30 years, there has been a subtle shift in emphasis from age to beauty. Nowadays, the aesthetics of a bonsai have come to be regarded as more important than how old it is. You could say that this is in part the result of Western culture, in which age and tradition are not held in such high regard as in the East. Beauty and ability have replaced seniority and experience right across the board.

The bonsai fraternity therefore finds itself in a dilemma. Is age no longer important, or should it still be regarded with awe? Perhaps the best answer is that age, although still important, is no longer the

PLANT SIZES

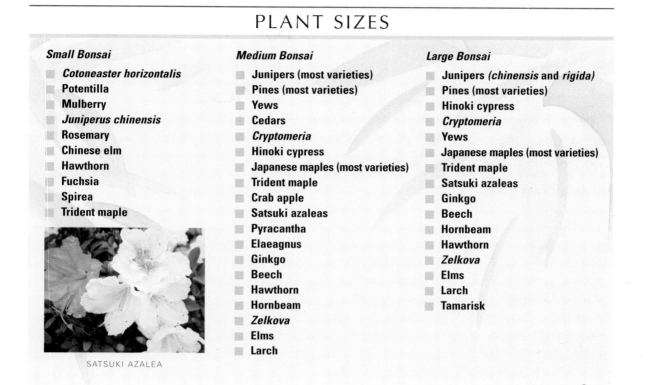

Small Bonsai

- *Cotoneaster horizontalis*
- Potentilla
- Mulberry
- *Juniperus chinensis*
- Rosemary
- Chinese elm
- Hawthorn
- Fuchsia
- Spirea
- Trident maple

SATSUKI AZALEA

Medium Bonsai

- Junipers (most varieties)
- Pines (most varieties)
- Yews
- Cedars
- *Cryptomeria*
- Hinoki cypress
- Japanese maples (most varieties)
- Trident maple
- Crab apple
- Satsuki azaleas
- Pyracantha
- Elaeagnus
- Ginkgo
- Beech
- Hawthorn
- Hornbeam
- *Zelkova*
- Elms
- Larch

Large Bonsai

- Junipers (*chinensis* and *rigida*)
- Pines (most varieties)
- Hinoki cypress
- *Cryptomeria*
- Yews
- Japanese maples (most varieties)
- Trident maple
- Satsuki azaleas
- Ginkgo
- Beech
- Hornbeam
- Hawthorn
- *Zelkova*
- Elms
- Larch
- Tamarisk

prime consideration. It is certainly not something that a bonsai owner should boast about. Great age is implied, never stated. Certain qualities of good bonsai, such as bark texture, trunk taper, root spread, and branch structure only come with advancing years—if not hundreds of years, then at least 30 or 40 years.

Size

The size of a bonsai is largely determined by convention and sheer practicality. In China and Japan, commercially traded bonsai range from small (6–12 inches/15–30 cm) to medium (12–24 inches/ 30–60 cm) to large (up to 4 feet/1.2 m). The Chinese are also fond of extremely large bonsai, which are displayed in parks and public gardens. These bonsai, grown in large ceramic or marble pots, may be as tall as 15 feet (4.5 m). Needless to say, they are

extremely old and rare. Such bonsai have a presence and aura that other bonsai do not possess.

Shohin

In countries where space is at a premium and many people live in high-rise apartments, smaller bonsai are the only practical option. This is one of the reasons why traditional, larger bonsai are becoming less popular in Japan. The trend now is for "shohin," or small bonsai. The most highly priced are 3 feet (90 cm) or smaller because these trees can be entered in competitive exhibitions where the maximum display width is 6 feet (1.8 m); which is the size of the tatami, the Japanese floor mat.

The Japanese trend is unlikely to influence Western preferences, because in the West, average gardens are much bigger and large bonsai can be displayed without much difficulty.

POTS AND CONTAINERS

A container of some kind is integral to any bonsai, which is by definition "a tree in a pot." The pot serves both a physical and an aesthetic function. By confining the roots of the tree within the pot, its vigor is restrained and the bonsai retains its miniature quality. At the aesthetic level, the shape, color, size, and texture of a pot can completely transform a bonsai's character.

 The history of bonsai containers stretches as far back as the Chinese civilization itself, and there are extant examples of bonsai pots that date back to the Tang dynasty (618–907 CE). The potteries at Yixing, Fukien, and Guandong in China, and at Tokoname, Yama aki, and Bizen in Japan have long been renowned for their wares and continue to produce high-quality bonsai pots today.

Choose your pot carefully

The choice of bonsai pot is based largely on convention, but is also determined by the grower's aesthetic sense. The human eye is a good judge of what is appropriate as far as size and scale are concerned. However, the ability to choose the right pot according to artistic merit is a skill that can take years to acquire.

Most of the ordinary bonsai that you buy from bonsai nurseries are planted in mass-produced Japanese or Chinese pots. There is nothing wrong with these containers, but if you are a serious hobbyist and have a special tree, it deserves something better. A good-quality pot was typically handmade in Japan or China. Some more expensive bonsai come planted in these high-quality containers. If you are lucky and know what to look for, you may come across a tree in a Tokoname or Yixing pot.

Quality pots

Antique Chinese bonsai containers are highly prized because they enhance the appearance and character of a tree. Most of the famous exhibition trees at major Japanese bonsai exhibitions are displayed in these containers. Owners of precious antique pots often hire them out to exhibitors.

The rapid growth of interest in bonsai in the West has given rise to a new breed of potters in Europe and North America who are making some exquisite pots especially for bonsai. These pots will in due course become collectors' items in their own right. Modern esoteric pots are also emerging on the bonsai scene—this shows that bonsai is a living art that is evolving all the time.

An avant-garde pot shaped like a pelvis. The tree and pot complement each other.

SECRETS OF SUCCESS

Many of the bonsai that are exported from Japan are sold at bonsai auctions. The enthusiasts who owned them in the past would have been sure to use good-quality pots. Have a close look at them: some may be as valuable as the trees themselves. Choose pots that have a patina because this signifies age, and an old or semi-antique container will add value to your bonsai. If the tree is Japanese and good quality, there is a good chance that the pot is a Tokoname. A seal makes the pot and the tree that much more valuable. A hand-engraved signature accompanying the seal further increases the bonsai's value, because that indicates it was made by a famous master potter.

CLOCKWISE FROM BOTTOM LEFT
Large Yixing pots from China; detail showing the decoration; maker's seal on a high-quality Japanese pot; detail of pot feet in the cloud pattern; detail of pot rims.

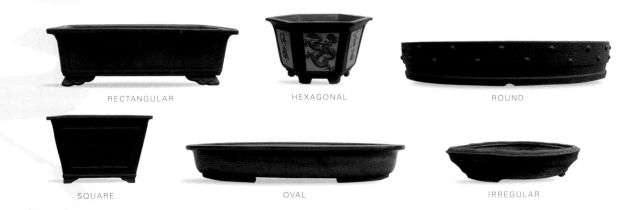

RECTANGULAR HEXAGONAL ROUND

SQUARE OVAL IRREGULAR

Pots come in a range of shapes, sizes, and colors, which can make choosing hard. Bonsai artists have formulated a set of principles over the years to help people select a pot according to particular style, species, and tree size. Deep pots are used for trees with thick trunks; shallow pots for those with slender trunks; very deep pots are used for Cascade and Semi-cascade trees. Use these rules as a general guide only: some of today's most inspiring examples of bonsai break the existing conventions.

Texture and glaze

Evergreens are usually planted in unglazed brown, gray, or dark-colored pots. Deciduous trees are usually planted in glazed pots. The texture of the clay body also has an important bearing: rough-textured or antique-looking pots are ideal for old trees, while the smoother-textured pots suit colorful, younger trees.

Lip shape and feet

The lip of a bonsai container can be wide, narrow, outward pointing, inward pointing, soft in appearance, or hard and rugged looking. The shape has a subtle but important influence on the mood or "feel" of the pot and therefore the tree.

Like the lip, the feet of a pot also have an important bearing on its character. Cloud feet (see page 61) imply formality, while plain feet are much more casual.

SHAPE GUIDE

Pot	Tree style
Rectangular	Powerful-looking and chunky trees
Round	Feminine and dainty-looking trees, round incurve pots and straight-sided pots are ideal for Literati trees
Oval	Forest plantings (groups of individual trees) and trees with sinuous curves
Square	Literati trees
Hexagonal and octagonal	Literati trees and trees with a symmetrical silhouette
Irregular	Windswept trees and trees with a significant driftwood component

MATCHING STYLE TO POT

Style	*Recommended pot*
Formal upright	Medium-to-deep rectangular or oval, depending on trunk thickness
Informal upright and Coiled	Medium-to-deep rectangular, oval, or round, depending on trunk thickness
Slanting	Medium-depth rectangular or oval
Windswept	Medium-depth rectangular or modern primitive (a particular style of asymmetrical rough-looking pot); unglazed and preferably rough textured
Cascade and Semi-cascade	Deep square, hexagonal, round, or octagonal
Literati	Medium-depth circular drum or incurve (pots with inward-curving sides); alternatively, square, hexagonal, or primitive; unglazed
Broom	Medium-to-shallow oval or round
Weeping	Medium-depth. Shapes as for Cascade
Root over rock	Medium-to-deep rectangular, oval, or round
Split trunk and Driftwood	Medium-to-deep rectangular or modern (unconventional); unglazed
Exposed root	Medium-to-deep, rectangular, round, hexagonal, or octagonal; unglazed
Twin, Triple, and Multiple trunks	Same criteria as Informal upright, although shallow pots are also suitable for slender trunks
Root connected and Raft	Medium-to-shallow rectangular, oval, or stone slab
Forest	Shallow oval or stone slab
Landscape	Shallow oval, rectangular, or stone slab; unglazed

ROUND HANDMADE BRITISH POT

SQUARE CASCADE JAPANESE POT

ANTIQUE CHINESE POT

COLOR

Flowering and fruiting bonsai have a charm all their own. They certainly add color and interest to a bonsai collection. You can also extend the period of interest by choosing species that flower at different times of the year. Apricot, forsythia, quince, and crab apple are early flowering trees, followed by wisteria, hawthorn, and Satsuki azalea. Then, in the fall, there are the bonsai grown for their colorful fruit. You can enjoy a great wealth of color when you include flowering and fruiting bonsai in your collection.

Good examples of bonsai, or "specimens," are highly prized. The features that make them so valuable are qualities such as a strong root base; gnarled and old trunks; dense, twiggy branches; and if is it a flowering or fruiting species, this is an added bonus. Pomegranate, which have gnarled and interesting trunks, are very rare and consequently command high prices. Good Satsuki azalea specimens are also extremely valuable. The value of unique specimens is a different matter entirely. Here, the price is only secondary. If an enthusiast wants a tree badly enough, he will find a way of buying it.

Color

Color is regarded as part of the total bonsai package, on a par with the trunk, branches, and leaves. Maples, which may be grown for their color alone, present a kaleidoscope of ever-changing hues. The varieties that begin as green in spring—when other maples are a bright red—eventually turn to scarlet in the fall, when the reds have taken on a softer shade. Even the evergreen conifers display a variety of different shades as their needles emerge and mature through the year.

The hue of a tree is dependent to a large extent on how it has been grown. The chemical makeup of the fertilizer can also affect a tree's color quite dramatically. A high-N (nitrogen) fertilizer applied in spring will make the leaves bright green, whereas high-P (phosphorus) and high-K (potassium) fertilizers applied in midsummer will induce good fall tints of red and gold, as will exposure to full sun throughout the growing season.

Fertilizers can also affect the flowering and therefore the fruiting capacity of trees. It is well known that fertilizers rich in P and K induce flower buds to form and that is why it is so essential to apply a high-P-and-K fertilizer to flowering subjects in summer. Different fertilizers can therefore affect bonsai in different ways. Every grower has his or her own favorite recipe for success. If you follow the packet directions for fertilizers, you won't go far wrong.

A Satsuki azalea in full bloom. There are thousands of varieties— this one is "Yama-no-hikari" with multicolored flowers.

COLOR FROM FLOWERS AND FOLIAGE

By choosing the right species of plant, you can have a very colorful display of bonsai throughout the year. Some trees, such as the Japanese maple, are grown for their colorful foliage; some, like the Satsuki azalea, are grown mainly for their flowers; while others have the bonus of both flowers and fruit.

CLOCKWISE FROM BOTTOM LEFT Different varieties of Japanese maple in early spring; Japanese maple 'Asahi Zuru' in its fall color; Satsuki azalea; Camellia; Pomegranate.

5

GROWING
SECRETS

*"By observing nature, we get to
understand how plants grow."*

THE BASICS

You do not need a degree in horticulture to grow bonsai successfully. As long as you carry out basic horticultural tasks such as watering and pruning, your tree will survive. However, if you can carry out these same jobs with a professional touch, you will notice a marked difference in the way your bonsai respond. The secrets revealed in this chapter, discovered over years of trial and error, will enable you to move above the rank of amateur. Once your horticultural skills become second nature, you will be free to explore the artistic side of bonsai.

 All living things require water, light, air, and nutrients. The ordinary plants in the garden come by these naturally. Bonsai, on the other hand, are confined to relatively small containers so they are much more demanding. The way you go about providing bonsai with their fundamental needs forms the basis of bonsai horticulture.

Light

Light is the energy source that powers photosynthesis, the process whereby a plant obtains food. Sunlight is best, but artificial light will perform the same function. The amount of light a bonsai receives is completely within our control. Depending on the needs of the plant, you can place your bonsai in full sun or partial or deep shade. Getting to know how much light each variety or species needs is critical to the health of the bonsai.

Water

Trees and plants obtain water through their root system. The roots penetrate the soil and seek out moisture, sometimes traveling great distances to do so. A bonsai's roots are confined to a pot, so the plant relies on us to provide water in the correct amount and at the correct frequency and times of day. How that water is applied is an art in itself. Such is the sophistication of the correct bonsai watering techniques that Japanese bonsai growers say it takes a lifetime to learn.

Air

Few people appreciate the role that air plays in the physiology of plants. Carbon dioxide is absorbed from the air through the leaves and combines with water to produce starch and sugar to feed the plant, using the energy of the sun's rays. Roots also need air, although it is used in a different way. Water and nutrients are absorbed by the fine root hairs that grow at the tips of the roots. The root hairs can only absorb water in the form of water vapor, and vapor is produced only if air is present. If the soil is flooded or becomes so compacted that air is excluded completely, the roots cannot take up moisture and the tree will die. A good bonsai soil is one that allows air to flow through it freely.

Bonsai need constant care and regular grooming to remain in good condition. Tended properly, a bonsai may outlive its owners.

SECRETS OF SUCCESS

Water, light, air, and nutrients are the four key ingredients for successful bonsai growing. It is important to understand how each of these factors works and how to provide it. Success does not depend on one single element—all four are essential. Different species have different needs and preferences as to the type of soil, and amounts of water, sunlight, and nutrients. These are explained, where necessary, in the appropriate sections of this book.

Nutrients

All plants and trees require nitrogen, phosphorus, and potassium—these are referred to as N-P-K. Nitrogen ensures strong, leafy growth; phosphorus promotes root growth; and flowers and fruit depend on potassium. The other basic nutrients required for plant life are calcium and magnesium, which usually occur in the soil naturally.

If soil is deficient, nutrients can be added in the form of fertilizer. The nutrients that are most often deficient are NPK, so most fertilizers aim to replace these three elements. They usually contain trace elements, such as magnesium, iron, boron, copper, and zinc, which are not needed in large quantities but which are essential for healthy growth. Fertilizer can be organic (derived from natural sources such as plants or animals) or inorganic (chemical-based). Both types are effective and used extensively by farmers and plant growers. Careful use of fertilizer to ensure your bonsai receives nutrients in the right quantities can make all the difference between a healthy and a sickly tree.

Pests and diseases

Keeping your bonsai free from harmful pests and diseases will ensure the tree's survival. This requires constant vigilance because problems can strike at any time. Knowing how to deal with pests and diseases in a safe manner is an essential part of bonsai horticulture *(see pages 156–165).*

Bonsai is not just about making miniature trees—it entails maintenance and grooming to ensure that they remain in pristine condition. Here, Indonesian bonsai master Robert Steven cares for his trees.

SOIL AND GROWING MEDIA

Soil is the vehicle by which air and water are carried to the roots. If the vehicle malfunctions or is defective, the tree will suffer. If the vehicle runs smoothly, the tree will maintain its perfect condition. While ordinary earth or loam is perfectly adequate for plants that grow in the ground, bonsai—if they are to thrive—require a more finely tuned soil structure.

 In order for roots to breathe and take up moisture, the soil particles must have spaces between them that allow air and moisture to flow through. If the spaces become blocked, the soil will not function efficiently. When a tree has been growing in a pot for a long time, the roots can clog up the air spaces, and the tree will deteriorate. Similarly, if a bonsai stands in water, the air spaces will become blocked and the roots will not be able to breathe and will eventually rot away. The first requirement for a good bonsai potting soil is its ability to let air and water flow through it. This is why soil particle size is so important.

A healthy bonsai will produce a mass of roots, like this, but will eventually deteriorate if air and water cannot penetrate the root ball.

Because the moisture that the roots absorb is taken in as water vapor and not in the form of liquid, the soil particles need to be able to hold just enough water to generate a vapor but not so much as to drown the roots. The ideal soil structure is one that is able to drain and hold sufficient water at the same time. How this is achieved has been the subject of extensive research by bonsai growers. The results of this research are the specially formulated soils from Japan, such as Akadama.

Akadama

In recent years, a Japanese growing medium called Akadama, or "red clay soil," has become widely available in the West. It is a clay subsoil that is mined commercially in central Japan and then processed and graded by particle size. Soil with particles of $\frac{1}{25}$–$\frac{1}{12}$ inch (1–2 mm) is sold as "very fine," while $\frac{1}{8}$–$\frac{1}{4}$ inch (3–6 mm) is "standard." Akadama has a neutral pH of about 6 and contains virtually no organic matter. Although clay-based, the particles are granular in structure. What is most unusual about the granules is that they retain their structure even after three or four years. The other great merit of Akadama is its ability to simultaneously drain and hold sufficient moisture. This is why it makes an ideal medium for most bonsai.

SECRETS OF SUCCESS

The traditional medium used in the West is based on varying proportions of loam, peat, and sand. This works well, but modifications using new ingredients have greatly improved bonsai soils. Finer-grain Akadama and bark chips make excellent loam and peat substitutes, and fired clay granules and pumice can be used instead of sand.

DRAINAGE LAYER

You don't need to create a drainage layer for bonsai up to 15 inches (38 cm) tall, but anything larger will benefit from a layer of coarse particles at the bottom of the pot. These prevent the soil from clogging drainage holes and encourage water and air to flow freely. Charcoal is a useful additive in the drainage layer.

However, Akadama is suited mainly to conditions in central Japan, which has heavy rainfall in summer and moderately cold temperatures in winter. Because the soil drains well, it does not get waterlogged easily and therefore reduces the risk of the root ball freezing solid in the winter. Although Akadama is often used neat—not mixed with other ingredients—in central Japan, around the Tokyo area, in other areas of the country where climatic conditions are different, Akadama is mixed with other ingredients to suit the local growing conditions. In the south, for instance, where temperatures are higher and rainfall is heavier, extra-coarse river sand is added to improve drainage.

In North America, northern Europe, and the Mediterranean countries, Akadama usually needs to be mixed with other ingredients, such as bark, grit, baked clay, and pumice in order to achieve the right balance of moisture retention and drainage. A smaller grain size holds moisture better, so you can also alter the balance by

A good bonsai medium should hold sufficient water but drain freely, so the ingredients should be granular in structure.

adjusting the proportion of finer and larger grains. If you sift the ingredients with the appropriately sized sieve, you can create the size of soil particle that will best suit your climate and size of tree. Although Akadama can be used on its own, it is best to mix it with other ingredients.

Bonsai soil

There is no such thing as a "universal" bonsai soil. Each soil should be tailor-made for the environment in which it is to be used and adapted according to tree species. Bonsai that grow in areas of heavy rainfall need a soil that drains quickly, while those suited to drier climates will benefit from a soil that holds moisture for longer. Pines and junipers prefer slightly drier conditions, which means a free-draining medium is the most suitable, whereas fruiting and flowering bonsai benefit from a mix containing more loam and organic matter.

A good bonsai medium drains freely. Soil particles that are too fine will eventually clog up the roots and prevent the water from draining properly. Any fine dust in a medium should be discarded. The smallest particle size should be $\frac{1}{25}$ or $\frac{1}{12}$ inch (1 or 2 mm), and the largest no more than $\frac{1}{5}$ or $\frac{1}{4}$ inch (5 or 6 mm). Soil with fine particles is more suitable for small bonsai, while larger particles suit larger trees. Specialist bonsai sieves that enable you to sift the soil to desired particle size are available.

Some of the indoor bonsai that originate in southern China are planted in a clay soil that resembles pottery clay. This may function adequately as a growing medium in parts of China where it is humid and wet for most of the year, but in a dry temperate environment, a soil with a more open texture is preferable.

How reliable is ready-made bonsai soil?

Ready-made Japanese soil such as Akadama is an excellent bonsai medium. Try it on its own first to see how it performs. If you're not satisfied with the result, experiment by adding varying amounts of an organic medium or sand to get the levels of retention and drainage exactly right. Beware of soil that is sold as bonsai media by general nurseries and garden centers. The product is often plain peat-based soil mix, attractively packaged. If it doesn't have a granular structure or any grit content, make your own instead or buy specialist soil from a bonsai nursery.

It is best to mix the soil to suit particular species, using one of the recipes shown opposite.

72

Basic ingredients for bonsai soil. **TOP ROW, LEFT TO RIGHT** Potting grit, fine tree bark, calcined clay particle (⅛–¼-inch/3–6-mm size). **BOTTOM ROW, LEFT TO RIGHT** Akadama (⅛–¼-inch/3–6-mm size), Kanuma soil, Heuga gravel.

SOIL MIX RECIPES

SOIL COMPONENTS	SOIL TYPES					
	General mix	Deciduous mix	Flowering mix	Pine	Juniper	Satsuki
Loam or Akadama, fine-to-medium grade	30%	40%	50%	20%	20%	-
Organic medium moss (coarse moss, peat, or fine bark)*	30%	30%	20%	30%	20%	30% (sphagnum moss)
Drainage medium (Heuga, Kirya sand, pumice, potting grit, Fuji sand) [any of these]	40%	30%	30%	50%	60%	70% (Kanuma soil)

* Organic matter substitutes may also include coconut fiber, mushroom compost, and finely chopped tree bark—especially pine bark.

GROWING FROM SEED

If you are considering bonsai as a hobby, buying a ready-made tree is a legitimate first step. But as you become more knowledgeable, you will begin to appreciate how much more there is to bonsai than simply admiring their beauty. For many people, the process of bonsai creation, rather than the "end product," is the essence of the art. It's true that some patience is required, but growing a tree from scratch and then caring for it over many years can bring a real sense of achievement.

 The key to growing from seed is to master the technique of seed sowing. Buy some seeds from a reputable seed supplier, preferably one that specializes in tree seeds. Alternatively, collect your own. Do this at the end of the fall to ensure the seeds are fully developed. Sow your tree seeds in seed flats or trays right away using a seed sowing medium— something like equal parts of peat and sand. Leave them out in an unheated greenhouse over the winter or alternatively, leave them outdoors, covered with a pane of glass. In the spring, the seeds should germinate. You need not worry too much about spacing when sowing the seeds because they will be transplanted into individual pots soon after they germinate.

Some tree seeds have a hard protective coat, which makes them more difficult to germinate. These seeds need to be soaked in water and placed in a plastic bag in a refrigerator to "stratify." Stratification is the process of alternate thawing and freezing that occurs in nature and that eventually breaks the dormancy of the seed. Some hard-coated seeds can take up to two years to germinate. So if they do not germinate in the spring immediately after sowing, leave them in their seed trays for another year and see if they sprout the following season.

Most varieties of maple seed prolifically when grown as garden trees. Each seed has the potential to grow into a tree one day.

"Bonsai seed" kits, which give the impression that you can produce a ready-made bonsai simply by sowing the seeds supplied in the kit, are misleading. Germination is only the first step in a very long process of bonsai creation. All these kits produce is ordinary seedlings that have to be carefully nurtured until big and strong enough to be shaped by wiring and pruning—this is assuming the seeds germinate in the first place. If the seeds are not fresh, they won't be viable. Leave these kits where they belong, on the shelf. It is far better to buy seeds from a reliable seed firm and plant them in the usual way.

BONSAI FROM SEED

❶ Freshly collected maple seeds being sown into a seed tray in late fall. They will remain in this seed tray all winter, where the action of alternate freezing and thawing will break their dormancy.

❷ In early spring, the seeds will germinate. Let them grow stronger for another three or four weeks, then transplant them into individual pots. Feed with a weak solution of liquid fertilizer every two weeks.

❸ Grow the seedlings in an unheated greenhouse. By summer, they should be at least 1 foot (30 cm) high. Each plant can grow as much as 2 feet (60 cm) in the first season if fed with the right nutrients.

SEED Q & A

Q How can I tell if a seed is fresh?

A Unfortunately, the only way to find out is to plant it. If a seed does not produce any seedlings, it is not fresh. Avoid the problem by always buying from a reputable seed company.

Q Is there a unique "bonsai seed"?

A No. The seed you get in so-called "bonsai kits" is just a plain seed. There is nothing special about it.

These Japanese maple seedlings are just a few months old. Each seedling was transplanted into a 3-inch (7.5-cm) pot after the first pair of leaves had formed.

GROWING FROM CUTTINGS

Propagating bonsai material from cuttings is perhaps as satisfying as growing from seed. It is also a fairly easy and quick method of raising good-quality plants at little or no cost. Other advantages are that you have full control over shaping right from the start and you can be sure that the plant will be true to type—unlike seedlings, which can be variable.

If you have a green thumb, you may decide to propagate your future bonsai from a cutting. This involves some gardening skills but doesn't need a special "bonsai" approach.

Many shrubs and trees propagate easily from stem and root cuttings. The secret is to know which plants will root by this method and how to achieve the best results. Not all plants will root from cuttings, so choose the right varieties. Of the ones that root from cuttings, some will root from softwood, some from semi-ripe wood, and others from hardwood. Each type of cutting entails a different process. Once you have produced a rooted cutting, the next step is to turn it into a bonsai by wiring and shaping.

Most deciduous and evergreen trees and shrubs propagate easily from semi-ripe wood cuttings. These are shoots that have grown in the spring and are just about to turn woody. You can use either a heel-cutting or a nodal-cutting, although the former is more successful. Hormone rooting medium—in powder or liquid form—can speed up the process, but is not really necessary. For hardwood cuttings of temperate varieties, it is necessary to use hormone rooting powder or liquid, although many tropical species such as bougainvillea and *Ficus* root easily without any rooting compound. Bottom heat can speed rooting but should be used with mist propagation or the cuttings will just dry out.

WHICH PLANT?

Deciduous species
Deciduous species that root easily from semi-ripe and hardwood cuttings include: cotoneaster, forsythia, berberis, Chinese elm, ginkgo, hornbeam, Japanese maple, and trident maple. Cuttings are best taken in early summer.

The ideal size for semi-ripe cuttings is 4– 5 inches (10–13 cm) long and about matchstick thick. For hardwood cuttings, you can use longer (up to 8 inches/20 cm long) and thicker material—up to $\frac{1}{4}$ inch (5 mm) in diameter. Evergreens such as Satsuki azalea and box *(Buxus)* also root easily from semi-ripe cuttings taken in early summer.

Conifers
Conifers that root easily include: all varieties of juniper, *Cryptomeria*, *Chamaecyparis* (Hinoki and Sawara cypresses), and yews. Conifers are best propagated from semi-ripe cuttings. Hardwood cuttings are not as successful. When the cuttings have rooted, let them develop for about a year before wiring and shaping them into bonsai.

HOW TO MAKE CUTTINGS

1 Ideal cutting materials are shoots that have grown in the current season. Choose a piece that is 4–6 inches (10–15 cm) long and about 1⁄16 inch (2 mm) thick. Remove the bottom leaves and cut the remaining leaves in half to reduce transpiration losses.

2 You can cut the leaves with a pair of sharp scissors. You should also remove the soft tip of the shoot because this would wilt anyway. Removing the tip will encourage the rooted cutting to bush from the dormant buds.

3 A well-prepared cutting should look like this—just a pair of leaves at the end of the shoot with four to six nodes.

4 Seed trays or flower pots are ideal for cuttings. The medium for rooting cuttings should be well drained, so a drainage layer of coarse material at the bottom is useful. Media for cuttings should also have sharp sand added to it.

5 Hormone rooting powder or liquid speeds up the rooting process. However, although useful, it is not absolutely essential. Most plant varieties will root quite readily without a hormone rooting material.

6 Insert the prepared cutting into the medium, leaving the top two leaves protruding out of the soil. You need to insert at least one-third of the stem into the soil. If you do not insert it deeply enough, the cutting could dry out.

BONSAI FROM SEEDLINGS AND CUTTINGS

Getting something to grow from seed and rooting a cutting are fairly straightforward horticultural tasks. These are jobs that even children can manage without much difficulty. How to turn the plants into bonsai is quite another matter. The secret is to grow the seedlings and cuttings into strong plants before attempting to convert them into bonsai.

 Determining when a young plant is at the right stage to make into a bonsai comes with experience, but the basic rule is to wait till the stem is firm enough to bend without snapping. After your seedlings have germinated, wait a few weeks for them to put out one or two pairs of leaves; then you can transplant them into individual pots and let them grow for a full year into strong plants. During that year, pinch out the growing tip to encourage the plant to become bushy.

You can do the same with cuttings so that they become bushier. If you wish to grow your seedling or cutting into a much taller plant, let it develop to the appropriate height before pinching out the tip.

BONSAI FROM SEEDLINGS

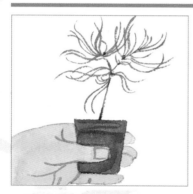

❶ Most conifer seedlings, such as pine and larch, are ideal subjects for wiring when fairly young. Do not wire seedlings that have just germinated—wait till they are fairly firm. If you wire when they are still soft, you risk snapping the stem.

❷ Seedlings that are matchstick thick are the right size for wiring. Insert a piece of aluminum wire about ¹⁄₁₆ inch (2 mm) in diameter into the soil and wire the stem up to the apex. Twist the wired stem into a tight S-shaped coil.

❸ Leave the wired seedling to grow and thicken in its pot for about a year. Remove the wire after a year. Then transfer it into a slightly larger pot and feed it at regular intervals with a weak general fertilizer.

BONSAI FROM CUTTINGS

❶ Young plants, such as this conifer cutting, will make instant bonsai with just a bit of wiring. Choose plants that are bushy and well branched, because this gives more options for low branches.

❷ Look at the plant carefully and decide which of the many branches you wish to retain for the final structure. The branches should be evenly distributed along the length of the trunk. Look at examples of good bonsai to guide you.

❸ Begin by wiring the trunk, using an appropriate grade of wire. Aluminum wire is best for young plants. Proceed to the branches, working from the bottom to the top. You can then transplant the tree into a bonsai pot.

RIGHT This young black pine grown from seed is just three years old. In the first year, the growing point was pinched out to stimulate side shoots. It was wired in the second and third years.

LEFT This Chinese juniper, from a cutting taken six years ago, was wired and shaped when it was three years old.

BONSAI FROM NURSERY MATERIAL

There are various ways you can create your own bonsai. If you have sufficient patience, you can choose to see the process through from the very start and grow your bonsai from a seed or a cutting. Alternatively, if you choose the right type of plant as your raw material, you can create a beautiful-looking bonsai in just a couple of hours from an established plant.

 Creating a bonsai from an ordinary tree or shrub that you buy from a nursery or dig up from your own or a friend's garden is probably the easiest way to get started in bonsai. Most nurseries or garden centers sell shrubs and trees that are already well established in containers or flower pots. The more mature these plants are, the better material they are for creating your own bonsai.

These junipers are typical of what you can find in nurseries and garden centers. They are ideal for bonsai because they are compact and have thick and gnarled trunks with lots of branches.

The varieties to look for are those that are most commonly used for bonsai. Of the deciduous trees, Japanese maples, American red maple, liquidambar, hornbeams, beech, birch, alder, elm, ginkgo, hackberry, oak, ash, cotoneaster, *Pyracantha*, crab apple, forsythia, *Berberis*, hawthorn, larch, and willow are just some of the popular varieties that can be used.

Evergreens include most pines, junipers, cedars, spruces, *Cryptomeria*, cypresses, elaeagnus, box, buttonwood, holly, and yew.

Look for bushy, well-formed plants: the more branches, the better. Look for plants that have short internodes—that is, with branches that are not too far apart. Gangly-looking plants are usually weak ones. And look for plants that have a thick trunk and good spreading roots. If you can find a plant with a trunk that looks gnarled and old, that is a bonus.

OTHER SOURCES

Raw material for bonsai can come from many sources—your own garden, friends' gardens, derelict building sites, and yards. You can get some lovely mature trees and shrubs that will make great bonsai.

ABOVE AND BELOW This is another sprawling juniper found in a garden center. All that was required was to plant the shrub in a bonsai pot, trim off the lower branches, and wire the branches into place.

ABOVE AND BELOW This San Jose juniper bonsai was made in just a couple of hours using the nursery shrub seen below. Half the branches were discarded in order to achieve this shape.

AIR LAYERING

Air layering is an ancient method of propagation practiced by the Chinese for thousands of years. It is still widely used because it is such an effective, quick way of producing mature plants. If done correctly, a new plant can be made in as little as three weeks. This can save years of growing time, and the precise shape can be obtained by selecting the right material.

 Over the centuries, different techniques of air layering have been devised to suit different species and situations. For instance, some varieties cannot be ring-barked completely, so the wire tourniquet method *(see page 84)* is used. Others will respond to any of the methods, although some methods may be slower than others.

Not all plants will air layer. As a guide, any plant that will root from cuttings will also air layer easily. Deciduous species include alder, beech, birch, box, elm, ginkgo, hornbeam, ivy, most maples, willow, and *Zelkova*. Flowering species include azalea, camellia, caragana, cherry, cotoneaster, crab apple, grape, hawthorn, jasmine, magnolia, peach, pear, pomegranate, potentilla, quince, spindle tree, viburnum, and wisteria. Coniferous species that will air layer include cedar, *Cryptomeria*, cypress, dawn redwood, juniper, larch, pine—only white and black pine, spruce, and swamp cypress.

RING BARK METHOD

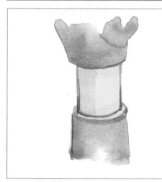

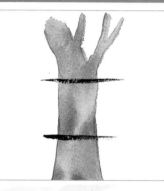

❶ The most common method is the "ring bark" technique in which a complete ring of bark is removed (above). Choose a branch that looks interesting—something that will resemble a bonsai once it has been severed from the parent plant.

❷ Using a marker pen, mark the two positions where you propose to cut into the bark so that the distance between them is little more than the thickness of the branch.

❸ Ring-bark the two points, using a sharp knife or box cutter. Be careful not to cut into the cambium layer (just below the bark) because this can cause the air layer to fail.

RING BARK METHOD

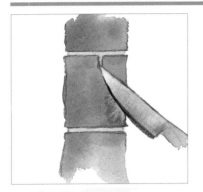

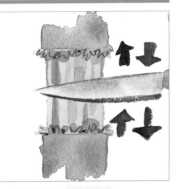

4 Using the knife, cut vertical slits between the two positions you have ring-barked, again making sure not to cut into the wood. Make as many vertical cuts as you need to—the object is to remove the bark between the two points.

5 Bark that is more than a couple of years old can be quite difficult to remove. However, the bark on some trees, including many of the tropical species such as *Ficus*, will come away easily, as shown here.

6 It is important to clean away all remaining traces of bark, using the knife or a piece of broken glass, for the air layering to be effective. Otherwise, the bark will not have been broken and nutrients will continue to flow up and down the branch as if nothing has happened.

7 Soak a ball of sphagnum moss in water, then place it around the cut portion. You can add a spoonful of diluted vitamin B solution or a proprietary Japanese reviving fluid to the moss to speed up root formation. Alternatively, apply hormone rooting powder or liquid to the cut surface.

8 Wrap the moss ball with polyethylene sheeting, tying it tightly at both ends. Clear polyethylene sheeting is adequate, although bubble wrap is even better because it holds the heat in the moss ball. Now all you have to do is wait a few weeks for the roots to appear.

9 When the root ball is full of roots, cut off the branch and pot it up in sphagnum moss or a peat mix. Be careful not to damage any roots. If you get heavy summer rainfall, leave the top of the plastic sheet open to catch the rain—this is removed when the air layering is put in the pot.

VARIATIONS ON AIR LAYERING

TOURNIQUET METHOD

This method is employed on species that do not take kindly to ring barking. The tourniquet needs to be as tight as possible to be effective. Copper or galvanized iron wire works best because it is not so prone to snapping when tightened.

CUTTING INTO BARK

In tropical countries, air layerings can be rooted by cutting into the wood. Earth or soil can be used as a rooting medium instead of sphagnum moss. Roots emerge in two to three weeks. Leaving the bark attached produces lovely surface roots.

MULTIPLE LAYERS

You can make several air layerings at the same time. Trees that air layer easily include *Ficus*, *Murraya*, *Acer japonicum*, and *Juniperus squamata*. In nurseries, dozens of air layerings are often made simultaneously without harming the "mother plant."

SECRETS OF SUCCESS

Timing is vital. Air layerings are best taken in the early spring in temperate and Mediterranean regions. If you live in a tropical climate, start the air layering just before the rainy season. Never start an air layering just before winter, because the tree will be dormant and won't produce roots till the following spring. It is also inadvisable to start an air layering in late summer because any emerging roots will not have enough time to mature. Furthermore, when you transfer the layering to a pot, it will not have sufficient time to produce enough roots to sustain the new tree.

When transferring the newly severed air layering into a pot, plant it in pure sphagnum moss rather than soil or a peat mix because moss encourages roots to develop at a much faster rate than soil. Take care not to disturb the moss ball. Don't be tempted to tease off the moss—you'll break the newly formed roots and the air layering will die.

These three air layerings were started in early May at the author's nursery. By late July, they had fully rooted. Bubble wrap was used to cover the moss balls. They are now ready to be severed from the parent plant. Branches up to 4 inches (10 cm) in diameter can be air layered in this way.

BRIDGE METHOD VARIATIONS

1 Sometimes the complete ring barking of a branch traumatizes the plant, resulting in failure of the air layering. Here, a window of bark is removed from each side of the branch, leaving two slivers of bark to act as bridges.

2 This variant of the bridge method involves the removal of two windows of bark but staggered as shown above.

3 In this variant, several slivers of bark are left as bridges to supply nutrients to the portion that is to be air layered. This multiple bridge method is often used on old conifers or when the branch to be layered is very thick.

4 Here, a vertical strip of bark, left behind to act as a bridge, is enough to sustain the portion being air layered and encourage roots to emerge.

SKIRT-STYLE AIR LAYERING

1 This is the "skirt" method, in which slivers of bark are cut but not removed, from the branch. Instead, they are peeled back. Sometimes the remaining bark pieces develop into roots and can make good surface roots for the potential bonsai.

2 A variant on the skirt method in which two coils or rings of wire are used. One is placed under the slivers of bark to prevent the bark from healing over and another is tied around the lip of the lower portion to prevent excessive callusing.

REPOTTING

Repotting, or "transplanting" as it is known in Japan, is probably one of the most misunderstood practices in bonsai. It is vital in the care of bonsai and must be done correctly. It is important to repot your bonsai regularly, or it will eventually start to fail. For a bonsai to remain in good condition, its soil needs to be changed, its roots need to be trimmed, and its branches need to be cut at regular intervals. Repotting your bonsai is like servicing your car regularly.

 One common bonsai myth is that a tree remains dwarf by a process of starvation and regular root pruning. In fact, the object of bonsai horticulture is a healthy tree, and root pruning is simply part of the repotting process. If a bonsai is left to grow indefinitely in the same pot, the roots become pot-bound, meaning no air or water can penetrate the soil and the tree will eventually die from not being able to take up nutrients. With the passage of time, the old soil breaks down, and other debris from fertilizer and dust clogs up the spaces between the soil particles, making it

The ideal time for repotting deciduous trees in temperate areas is in the early spring when the new buds are just beginning to swell.

impossible for fine roots to grow. Trimming a bonsai's roots every two or three years and changing the soil rejuvenates the tree by giving its roots room to develop.

In temperate areas, early spring is the best time to repot deciduous trees, but don't go simply by the calendar: study the tree and watch it carefully for signs of new life. Start repotting when the dormant buds are just about to swell. With so much latent energy waiting to be unleashed, any cuts made to the roots will soon heal, and new roots will grow quickly.

Some Japanese books and magazines recommend repotting flowering trees such as quince, crab apple, and apricot after flowering. In northern Europe and North America, this is inadvisable, because it means repotting in very late spring or early summer. It is better to repot flowering subjects in very early spring—February or early March in cool temperate regions—and protect them from hard frost after repotting.

Emergency repotting
If you have to repot because the pot is broken in a storm, put the tree in a slightly larger pot as a temporary measure and wait till the following spring to repot it properly. Don't be tempted to tease or cut the roots in the middle of summer or in the depths of winter. These are not the best times to repot.

HOW OFTEN SHOULD YOU REPOT?

There is no hard-and-fast rule when it comes repotting. Do it when the bonsai needs it. Check by taking the bonsai out of its pot and examining its roots. If the roots fill the pot completely, it is time to repot. If there is still some space left for the roots to grow, it can remain in the same pot for another year. Fast-growing trees, such as the trident maple, may need repotting annually. Older trees grow at a slower rate than younger ones, so can be repotted less frequently. Trees that grow in the Tropics are more vigorous than those that grow in temperate regions, so their root system develops much faster and annual repotting is the rule rather than the exception.

The roots on this tree are really pot-bound—which means that very little water or air is able to penetrate the soil. It is time the tree was repotted.

SATSUKI AZALEA

Satsuki azalea is the only bonsai that can safely be repotted in summer. In Japan, it is standard practice to repot Satsukis after flowering, at the end of June or early July. In Europe and North America, this can be risky if the weather is hot and dry. The end of February or early March is usually a safer option.

These Satsuki azaleas are being repotted in mid-June in Japan, just before the rainy season—this is the only bonsai that can be repotted in summer.

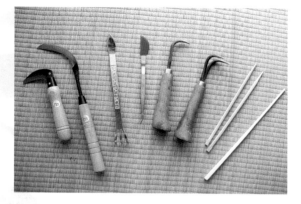

From left—two sickles for cutting around the edge of the root ball prior to removing the tree from its pot. Rake/spatula and spatula/tweezer for teasing out roots and prizing the root ball out of its pot. Root hooks for teasing out roots. Chopsticks for teasing out roots.

Soil scoops for shoveling soil into the bonsai pots during the final stages of repotting. This saves having to handle soil with your bare hands. Set of sieves for grading and sieving soil. Sieves are crucial for achieving the correct size of soil particles.

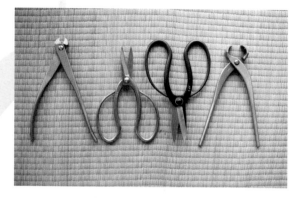

Bonsai wire cutter. This tool has been specially developed for cutting bonsai wire and for removing wire from trunks and branches. It is superior to any another type of wire cutter. The large handle scissors are used for cutting the roots after they have been teased out, and the root cutter is used for cutting thick roots that scissors cannot handle.

Coco brush for cleaning the soil surface. Jin pliers for stripping bark and removing wires. Drainage mesh for covering the drainage holes in bonsai pots. Dibblers for pushing soil into the root crevices during repotting. The dibblers here are a piece of bamboo stick and chopsticks of different sizes.

How to repot

If the roots are tightly packed and crammed against the side of the pot—for an example of this, see the photograph on page 87—the tree is potbound and it is time for it to be repotted.

Repotting involves five steps—taking the tree out of its pot; teasing the roots; cutting the excess roots; putting the tree back in its pot; and filling it up with fresh soil. Repotting is not a complicated process and should not take long—between 5 and 20 minutes, depending on the size of the tree. The mechanics are fairly straightforward, but timing is absolutely crucial because the weather window for doing this is relatively short.

TAKING A TREE OUT OF ITS POT

① Getting the tree out of its pot is the first task. This could be difficult if the tree has been growing in the same pot for many years because the roots will be tightly packed around the edges. This special sickle cuts the roots from the sides.

② After cutting the roots with the sickle, you still need to pry the tree out of the pot. A useful tool for this purpose is the rake-spatula. Using the spatula end, push the blade into the pot and lever the root ball gradually out of its pot.

③ Once the root ball is free, take the tree out and examine it for any signs of root rot or damage from insects and other pests.

SECRETS OF SUCCESS

Newly potted trees should not be exposed to extremes of temperature or to drying winds. Put them in a cool, unheated greenhouse or similar environment. Water the soil so that it remains damp but does not become soaking wet. Wait at least a month before applying a weak solution of fertilizer to prevent its burning the tips of the newly cut roots. When the new leaf buds start to open, continue to keep the tree protected from strong sunshine, drying winds, and frost.

Bonsai that have old crusty bark need to be handled with great care when repotting. Be careful not to damage the bark—it has taken decades to grow.

DEALING WITH ROOTS

1 If the roots are coiled around in the pot, you can loosen some of them with your fingers. Shake off any debris such as drainage mesh and tying wires that might have gotten lodged in the root ball.

2 You can now proceed to tease out the root ball using either a root rake or a single- or double-pronged root hook. Tease by pulling the roots outward in a radial fashion. Remove at least 1 inch (2.5 cm) of the root ball.

3 Using a pair of root-cutting scissors or shears, cut away the roots until they resemble stubble around the exposed root ball.

PREPARING THE POT

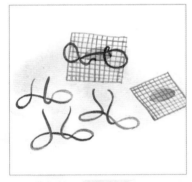

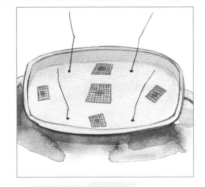

1 Cut square or rectangular pieces of drainage mesh and twist pieces of wire, as shown above, to anchor the mesh into the drainage holes.

2 Place the pieces of mesh over the drainage holes and secure them fast by twisting the wire ends. Pass two pairs of wires through the tying holes, leaving the ends long enough to tie around the trunk.

3 For medium- and large-size bonsai, a drainage layer of larger soil particles is fairly important. Some people do not bother with a drainage layer at all, but it does facilitate drainage and results in a healthier tree.

FINISHING OFF

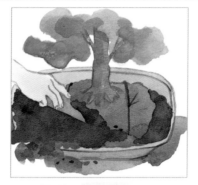

1 Place the tree in the pot on top of the drainage layer and tie the root ball in position, using the pair of wires that were threaded through the tying holes. Use a pair of pliers to tighten the wires.

2 Once the tree is tied in position, fill up the pot with bonsai soil using a soil scoop as shown.

3 Fill up all the soil crevices using a chopstick or dibbler, so there are no large voids. Press firmly with the dibbler. Water the tree using Vitamin B solution or a proprietary Japanese reviving fluid—these are not obligatory, but help to establish roots quickly.

This Hinoki cypress has just been repotted into a large oval pot. It was in a much smaller rectangular pot prior to repotting. The larger pot is far better suited to the cypress from both the aesthetic and horticultural standpoint.

WHAT IF I FORGET TO REPOT?

If you forget to repot or run out of time, don't worry, the tree will not die. Just wait until the next year, and in the meantime, check after watering to ensure that the roots are able to take up water *(see pages 96–97)*. Continue to feed in the normal way. If your tree is very pot-bound, drilling holes through the root ball *(see page 96)* will facilitate watering.

FERTILIZING

Because bonsai trees grow in small pots, you need to apply fertilizer from time to time to ensure that they receive sufficient nutrients. There are many bonsai fertilizers on the market—organic, inorganic, or a mixture of both. Many proprietary potting soil mixes for ordinary garden use have fertilizer already mixed in, but it is better to use a bonsai soil mix without any added fertilizer. You can then apply fertilizer as and when the bonsai needs it, using the right type in the correct amount.

 Trees and plants normally have two spurts of growth: one in the spring and another in midsummer. To be most effective, apply fertilizer to coincide with these two periods. If you use a weak concentration, you can apply in monthly intervals from the spring until early fall. Never apply fertilizer in winter when the tree is dormant, because this will only stimulate the tree and expose new growth to damaging cold and frost.

Types of fertilizer

There are many bonsai fertilizers on the market—organic, inorganic, or a mixture of both. Fertilizer is available in solid or liquid form. Solid fertilizer can be bought as a powder, as granules, or as pellets. All fertilizers should state the NPK content on the packet (for example, 8-8-8). This tells you the percentage weight of active or soluble nitrogen, phosphorus, and potassium. Fertilizers for use in spring have a high nitrogen content, in the region of 8 or higher (8-8-8 or 10-10-10). A high nitrogen content encourages good leaf growth and your trees will look healthy and green. Lawn fertilizer has an especially high nitrogen content—sometimes as much as 17 percent—and is a good fertilizer for bonsai in the spring, particularly if it also contains trace elements.

Fertilizers for use in late summer or fall have a lower nitrogen content and a higher potassium and phosphorus content (for example, 4-10-10). The higher potassium and phosphorus content promotes root and bud formation for the following year. Fertilizers for roses, tomatoes, and fruiting trees have high P and K content and work well on bonsai.

Organic fertilizers

Japanese growers are fond of using rapeseed fertilizer, which contains fish meal and other trace elements. It is available as a powder or in pellets that you sprinkle on the surface of the soil. Natural fertilizers are very good for free-draining soils such as Akadama *(see page 70)* and river sand because they do not leach out so rapidly. However, they can give off a putrid smell because they ferment and they also encourage worms and other organisms, so be prepared to put up with this inconvenience.

Liquid and solid fertilizers

Most professionals choose solid fertilizer over liquid fertilizer for their outdoor trees because it is easier to control the amount that is applied. Liquid is usually more convenient for small indoor trees. It comes in a concentrated form, so it has to be diluted before use. It is more easily assimilated than solid fertilizer, but it has to be applied more often. Do not apply liquid fertilizer to outdoor bonsai in rainy weather, because it will only flow away.

SECRETS OF SUCCESS

Knowing how much to apply is the key to successful feeding. Don't be tempted to apply a huge dose of fertilizer in the hope of a quick result. Your bonsai can only take so much at a time. If you overfeed, you may even kill your bonsai.

Plastic fertilizer baskets are used to cover fertilizer pellets to prevent birds and animals from stealing them. The fertilizer leaches into the soil whenever it rains or the tree is watered.

Fertilizing dos and don'ts

Applying too much fertilizer can be more harmful than applying none at all. Always follow the manufacturer's instructions and apply only a small amount of fertilizer at a time. Never feed a sick or dying tree. Fertilizer will only make it worse. Sick trees require a different treatment. Fertilizer should be regarded as a food supplement rather than medicine. Fertilizers are not a remedy for bad horticultural practice.

SECRETS OF SUCCESS

- Apply fertilizer from spring onward and stop by early autumn.
- Use high N fertilizers in spring and high P and K fertilizers in late summer.
- Use fertilizers sparingly. Small doses at frequent intervals will be more effective than large doses once in a while.
- Older trees need less fertilizer than younger trees.
- Never feed deciduous trees until the new leaves have hardened.
- Never apply fertilizer in winter when trees are dormant.
- Don't feed flowering trees during and immediately after flowering. Wait a month before feeding.
- Don't feed newly potted trees until they are growing strongly.

REVERSE OSMOSIS

Plants absorb nutrients via their fine root hairs by a process known as osmosis. Osmosis can take place only if the nutrient solution in the roots is at a higher concentration than the nutrient solution in the soil. One of the risks of applying too much fertilizer is reverse osmosis, whereby the nutrient concentration in the soil becomes too strong. When this happens, the nutrients flow in reverse, out of the roots, causing the tree to dehydrate. In serious cases of overfeeding, the tree may even die. If you suspect you have applied too much fertilizer, immediately immerse your bonsai in a trough or large bowl of water overnight to allow the fertilizer to leach out from the soil.

CORRECTING REVERSE OSMOSIS

COARSE GROWTH FROM OVERFEEDING

AESTHETIC DISFIGUREMENT

Excessive feeding induces coarse growth, which can ruin the fine ramification of deciduous trees such as maples and *Zelkova*. Certain evergreens, such as pines, can also suffer from branch thickening if overfed. Pines in the Literati style *(see pages 55 and 111)* are particularly vulnerable. Trees of exhibition quality with fine ramification need careful attention. You should give just enough fertilizer to keep the trees green and healthy without inducing vigorous growth. Japanese rapeseed fertilizer is very good for this purpose.

ORGANIC FERTILIZER PELLETS

ORGANIC FERTILIZERS

Organic fertilizers, such as animal and poultry manure, should be used in moderation. Never use these fertilizers fresh. It is always best to leave them to stand for several months to decay and "cool off" before applying. Vegetable manure, or composted material, is safer, but is more useful as an ingredient for improving soil structure than as a fertilizer. The most effective organic fertilizers are rapeseed and fish emulsion, which can be used in conjunction with inorganic fertilizers for excellent results.

SOIL ACIDIFIERS

Certain plants, such as rhododendron and azalea, require acid soil conditions in order to thrive. If the soil is not acid enough, iron compounds in the soil cannot be released for the plant to absorb. Iron needs to be supplied to the plant in a form that it can absorb. When iron is deficient in a plant, its leaves turn yellow. Certain absorbable compounds called iron chelates will remedy this condition—they are sold under various proprietary names, including "soil acidifiers." When a plant is given this, sickly looking yellow leaves will become healthy and green. Acidifiers can also be used as a foliar spray on sick plants. Do not confuse yellowing fall leaves with iron deficiency! Satsuki azaleas, maples, and most evergreen conifers will benefit from a regular application of acidifier during the growing season.

IRON DEFICIENCY ON CAMELLIA

FALL LEAVES OF SATSUKI AZALEA

WHICH PLANT?

Do not apply fertilizer to deciduous trees, such as maples, until the new leaves have hardened. If you apply it when the leaves are soft, it can burn the tips, causing them to blacken. Evergreen trees start to grow much earlier than deciduous ones, so you can apply the fertilizer earlier, at the beginning of spring.

95

WATERING

Forgetting to water bonsai is one of the most common reasons for failure. Watering bonsai is a skill. Do it correctly and your trees will thrive; do it incorrectly and your trees will suffer. Some experts say it takes a lifetime to learn how to water correctly, but follow the guidelines here and you'll be headed in the right direction.

 The secret of good watering is knowing when to do it. You should water only when the soil is dry. You can usually tell when a bonsai is dry simply by looking at the soil surface and touching it with your hand. If the soil looks dry and feels dry, it is probably time to water. However, if the pot is particularly deep, the soil inside the root ball may still be damp. Test for dampness by dipping a wooden stick into the soil and seeing if it comes out wet.

If bonsai are left outside during the winter or early spring, they can become waterlogged during spells of heavy rain. If this is followed by very cold weather, the root ball can freeze, causing severe damage to the roots. You can reduce the risk of waterlogging by standing your bonsai pot on its edge to facilitate draining. If you have a pot-bound bonsai that is not draining properly, you can remedy the situation by drilling holes through the root ball. This will also allow air to penetrate.

WATERING METHODS

HOW TO WATER
When watering your bonsai, make sure you soak it thoroughly until the water runs out from the drainage holes.

STANDING ON EDGE
If bonsai are left waterlogged, they will suffer root rot, especially in the winter. If you stand the plant on edge, the water will drain away quickly.

DRILLING ROOT BALL
Bonsai that are badly potbound will not allow water to penetrate the root ball. You can alleviate the situation by drilling holes through the compacted root ball.

SECRETS OF SUCCESS

Here are some useful tips for watering your bonsai.

- The root ball should always feel damp—not soaking wet or bone dry.

- Allow the soil to dry out slightly between each watering, but don't let it dry out completely.

- During the summer, err on the side of caution and water your deciduous trees at least once a day. Don't let the soil stay bone dry for more than a couple of hours. Leaves shrivel very easily in hot, sunny weather.

Shriveled leaves result from poor watering

- In ordinary weather, watering once a day in the morning is sufficient. If you have to water twice a day, then morning and evening watering is ideal. In very hot weather, water in the afternoon as well.

- Don't water in the midday sun. If you have no choice, water the soil only and not the foliage.

- If you have to water more than once a day, let the soil dry before watering again.

- Don't water continually throughout the day.

- Don't rely on rain to water your bonsai. It is rarely enough.

- There isn't much advantage in using rainwater on your bonsai; tap water is perfectly acceptable.

- Don't use a fierce jet of water on the soil—it will wash away both fertilizer and soil. Water with either a watering can or a hose with a fine rose.

- Automatic watering systems can be useful, but check regularly to see that the system works properly. There is no substitute for hand watering: it is more accurate and not as wasteful.

- Water each tree for about 10 seconds, leave it for a couple of minutes and return twice more, repeating the watering for 10 seconds each time.

- Let the water fall gently on the entire tree.

- Concentrate the water on the soil so that the roots get most of the water.

- Don't water flowers when they are in bloom. Water only the soil.

- Check that the water has drained through the pot.

- Don't stand a tree in water permanently or the roots will rot.

- If you have to leave your trees for more than a day, make sure someone waters them for you. Give them clear instructions on how to water.

- If you go away on holiday, arrange for a "bonsai-sitter" to take care of your trees. Some nurseries offer a vacation-care service. It isn't a good idea to rely on rain to do the watering—there may not be any.

PINCHING AND PRUNING

The twin tasks of pinching and pruning serve two important purposes. First, they are the means by which the pads of foliage on the branches and overall silhouette are created, and second, they ensure that a bonsai appears well groomed. If you don't prune and pinch correctly, you will not achieve fine ramification and your bonsai will become unkempt and lose its shape.

Spring and early summer are the busiest times for pinching and pruning. As soon as the new shoots or buds appear, they need to be trimmed to develop the twig structure or keep the tree in shape. The precise timing will vary with the species and age of the tree.

Many newcomers to bonsai prune simply to retain the tree's silhouette. If you do this over the long term and never thin the inside, the tree will eventually become a tangle of crossing branches. The twigs inside the tree will suffer because light and fresh air will not be able to penetrate. A dense structure also creates an ideal breeding ground for pests and diseases.

Pinching and pruning increases ramification—the density or twigginess of the bonsai's branches. The principle is simple enough. By pinching out the growing point or tip of the new shoot, you force it to bud farther back. Pinching is done with the thumb and fingers—hence the expression. Pruning is normally done with long handle twig shears. When using shears, avoid cutting the foliage because this leaves brown marks. It is best to cut into the stem or wood. This is standard horticultural practice. The only difference

with bonsai is that you make a careful selection of the shoots you allow to develop so that you get precisely the shape your want.

This Chinese juniper forest was made in 1986—it is a large group and extremely vigorous. It requires constant pinching throughout the year and major pruning every alternate year.

PINCHING FOR ROUTINE MAINTENANCE

① The growing points of most plants will continue to extend unless they are pinched out. By removing the growing points, you will encourage density in the twig and branch structure.

② New shoots are usually soft and tender. You may either pinch, using thumb and forefinger, or prune with scissors or pruners. Either method is acceptable.

③ If you have a lot of shoots to pinch out, scissors might be more convenient than your thumb and forefinger. With deciduous trees such as beech or maple, it is a good idea to remove the top two leaves as you pinch so that light can penetrate the dense twig structure below.

The Chinese juniper forest before pruning.

④ By removing the growing point you are stimulating the dormant buds in the leaf axils to grow. In a matter of days, the new buds should start growing.

⑤ Pinching and pruning is best done in spring or summer, which is the growing season. If it is done in fall or winter, the new growth will not emerge until the spring.

99

HOW TO PINCH AND PRUNE DIFFERENT SPECIES

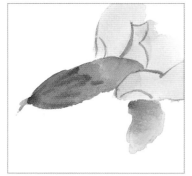

PRUNING CONIFERS
Firs *(Abies)* and spruces *(Picea)* have young growth that resembles brushes or foxes' tails, unlike the new leaves on deciduous trees. The new growth can be pruned with scissors.

PINCHING CONIFERS
Alternatively, it can be pinched, using your thumb and forefinger, as shown here. The new growth should be allowed to extend slightly before it is trimmed back. Allowing the new growth to develop lets the tree become stronger.

PRUNING A SPRUCE BRANCH PAD
This is how you should trim a branch pad of a spruce *(Piceas)*. Removing the tips encourages new buds to develop farther back into the branch structure. If the shoots were just allowed to grow, the branch pad would look very sparse.

PINCHING DECIDUOUS TREES
Beech, hornbeam, and other deciduous trees have soft young shoots. Pinch off the growth that extends beyond the existing silhouette. This stimulates the buds farther back to grow. Eventually you will also have to thin out the dense structure inside the tree.

PRUNING ALTERNATE LEAVES
Deciduous trees with alternate leaves should be pruned to an outward-pointing bud. Inward-growing shoots will make the structure too dense. Leave a stub about ¼ inch (6 mm) from the leaf axil. Pruning too close can cause dieback to the next node.

PINCHING AND PRUNING CYPRESSES
New growth on plants like Hinoki cypress (white cedar) and *Cryptomeria* has no distinct terminal shoots. Pinching and pruning simply involves removing all end growth. Hold the foliage with the thumb and forefinger and pluck away the shoots.

PINCHING AND PRUNING DIFFERENT SPECIES

PINCHING A NEEDLE JUNIPER
Prune *Juniperus rigida* (needle juniper) with scissors in spring to encourage new shoots to grow from within the twig area. In summer, pinch out new growth with thumb and forefinger, as shown, to maintain the shape.

REMOVING TERMINAL BUDS
Sometimes the terminal buds of the new growth from firs and spruces need to be removed to maintain the shape. Remove new growth as soon as it appears—break off the buds by twisting with your thumb and forefinger.

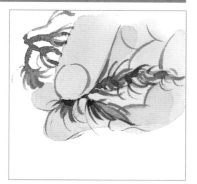

***CHINENSIS* AND *MEDIA* JUNIPERS**
Many junipers of the *chinensis* and *media* species produce growth like the above. If the shoots are soft, remove them by pinching. If they have become too hard, you will have to use scissors to prune.

PINCHING AND PRUNING PINES

❶ New shoots on pines are called "candles." In spring the shoots start to grow and become elongated. Candles often grow in clusters of two, three, four, or five. Keeping two is enough. When you have two candles, trim back the longer one.

❷ Trim the candles either by pinching with thumb and forefinger or by cutting with scissors. By removing the longer, and therefore stronger, shoot, you can control and balance the vigor of the shoot or branch.

CAN YOU OVERPINCH?

Exercise discretion. Never pinch or prune an unhealthy tree—this will make it weaker. If you don't let any new shoots or leaves grow on a healthy tree, the tree will get weak, because it will not get a chance to produce the food it needs. Also, constant pinching can make trees too dense, so that in time they need to be restructured to let in light and air and restore shape.

CARE THROUGH THE YEAR

Bonsai need constant care and attention. If you neglect them for even a short period, they will start to suffer. Use the following schedule as a guide to the different tasks you need to perform throughout the gardening year.

WINTER

- Prepare according to your local climate. If you typically experience very cold average minimum temperatures, such as 41°F/5°C, you will need to make careful arrangements for shelter *(see pages 104–105)*. Clean out your cold frames, basement, or greenhouses, or wherever you choose to shelter your bonsai. Consult your local bonsai club or dealer if you are unsure about what provision to make.

- Tropical and subtropical varieties must be taken indoors before the cold sets in.

- Avoid alternating spells of freezing and thawing, because this can upset the dormancy of hardy species.

- If you keep your bonsai under cover, make sure the soil is not allowed to dry out completely.

- Never feed bonsai at this time of year, even indoor bonsai.

- Pests and diseases thrive in winter quarters that are mild and damp, so be vigilant.

- Take stock of your trees, both physically and aesthetically. Now that the deciduous trees are bare, you can study the structure of the branches and see how you can improve them.

- Order soils and other accessories such as wire and tools.

This *Cornus officinalis* blooms in early February when most trees are still dormant. It is perfectly hardy in countries such as Britain and central Japan.

FALL

- Stop feeding by September.
- Continue to water until late October.
- Continue to watch for pests and diseases.

SPRING

- Your first task in early spring is to check that your bonsai have come through the winter safely. If the winter has been hard, check that the roots have not rotted and that the twigs and fine branches have not suffered damage.

- The next task is to check which of your trees need repotting. Repot deciduous trees first—as soon as the dormant buds begin to swell. Evergreens are usually repotted three or four weeks later. While repotting, take the opportunity to do some structural pruning before the trees begin to leaf.

- Have a thorough spring-cleaning. Clear out the dirt and debris from your greenhouse, cold frame, pot storage, and bonsai staging. Japanese nurseries spray lime-sulfur as a disinfectant, but you can use any proprietary disinfectant. Make sure you have enough new soil, wires, and other accessories.

- This is an ideal time to attend workshops and classes to learn more about bonsai. Bonsai nurseries also receive new trees from abroad in the spring, so it is a good time to buy.

- Evergreen bonsai should be given their first application of fertilizer in early spring.

- By late spring, the deciduous trees will need their first pruning and pinching.

SUMMER

- Bring any repotted trees out from their protective shelters.

- Regular watering starts now. In early summer, watering once a day should be sufficient, but as the season progresses and temperatures rise, increase to two or three times a day.

- Keep a close eye on insect pests and diseases and take remedial action as necessary (see pages 156–165).

- Prune and pinch regularly to keep your trees in good condition. With most species, this is almost a weekly task.

- Start feeding your deciduous trees as soon as the leaves have hardened—usually a month after they have emerged. Continue to feed on a regular basis: once a month for young developing trees but less frequently for major specimens to retain fine branch ramification.

- If you live in an area that is prone to storms, make sure you have somewhere to shelter your bonsai.

The author's nursery in the fall is a riot of color. The reds and golds of the maples are an exquisite sight.

PROTECTION FROM THE ELEMENTS

Each country's climate is different. Large countries such as the United States can have as many as five different climate zones—cool temperate, Mediterranean, desert, tropical, and subtropical. You need to know which zone you live in because it will be your guide to what bonsai you can and cannot grow successfully.

 Because bonsai are grown in containers, their roots are particularly vulnerable to extreme cold. Protecting your bonsai in winter is important for their survival. The degree of protection depends on the severity of the winters you experience. If you live in a mild temperate climate where minimum winter temperatures average around 32°F (0°C), your bonsai should not require special winter protection—putting your bonsai underneath its display benches should be adequate. Snow is not usually a killer in cool temperate areas; if anything, it acts like a blanket. Drafts and cold winds cause more damage because the windchill can stress the trees.

If you get a cold spell lasting more than two or three days during which the daytime temperature does not rise above freezing, put your bonsai under cover. Bring them out as soon as temperatures rise. Bonsai should not be kept in a shed or garage for long periods because they need light and moisture.

Some hobbyists keep their bonsai in unheated greenhouses during the winter. If you do this, be aware of the increased risk of alternate thawing and freezing during spells when the sun shines brightly. This can break a plant's winter dormancy, leading to vulnerable new shoots.

More elaborate winter protection will be necessary if you live in a cold temperate climate. This includes continental Europe, central Canada, the Midwest and the northeastern United States. In these regions, you need to protect your bonsai in special winter quarters.

SECRETS OF SUCCESS

If you live in a Mediterranean or subtropical climate, you have to provide protection only when frosts are forecast. Covering your bonsai with plastic sheeting or floating row cover fabric should be adequate. Shade tunnels are also very useful for frost protection in mild temperate and Mediterranean areas.

Winter quarters

Winter quarters can range from state-of-the-art greenhouses to makeshift shelters constructed from plastic sheeting. A sturdy greenhouse, which can be heated if necessary, is the ideal solution. Polyethylene tunnels are a good substitute, provided they are sturdy enough to withstand the weight of snow. If you do not have the space for such structures, moving your bonsai into the basement, shed, or garage during very cold spells can be just as effective. Hobbyists who live in milder regions bury their bonsai in the ground with just the trees

Even if you choose trees that suit your environment, there may be times in the year when you need to protect them.

above soil level. They then cover them over with mulch or plastic sheeting to give additional protection. An alternative is to dig a pit and fill it with peat and bury the pots in peat and then cover with plastic sheeting until the frosts are over. Those who live in regions that only have mild winters do not need to go to these lengths. Simply protecting their plants under shade structures will be quite adequate. In fact, Satsuki azaleas, pines, and junipers all benefit from protection under shade structures in winter because it gives their foliage a deep green color.

Summer protection

Fierce heat in summer can burn bonsai leaves. To prevent scorching, commercial growers use shade or lath houses, which can provide 30–60 percent shade. These simple structures are robust enough to withstand storms and strong winds. Do not place your bonsai in the shade throughout the summer because your trees need as much sunlight as possible. Use a shade house only when the sun is at its fiercest. All bonsai need sunlight to grow well, but don't let them get scorched in very hot weather.

6

DESIGN AND SHAPING PRINCIPLES

"In bonsai, the most beautiful trees are often those that have the simplest design."

THE COMPONENTS OF BONSAI DESIGN

Like any artistic work, a bonsai is a culmination of many different processes. The bonsai artist begins with an initial concept that is translated into a design and then realized in the bonsai's creation. This chapter takes you through the essential design and shaping processes. It covers the various techniques and the tools you will need to practice them.

CONCEPT AND IMAGE

First you need an idea of what you are trying to create. All bonsai start off as a concept. The tree you have in mind may be one you have seen in nature or an image remembered from a film or book. Like a model maker, the aim of a bonsai grower is to re-create that image of a full-size tree in miniature form.

BASIC SHAPE

The starting point for all bonsai design is a triangle—the shape of most trees in nature. The triangle may be equilateral, asymmetric, tall and thin, or squat and flat. It may be domed like a beehive, or taper to a point like a Christmas tree. Almost all styles in bonsai, including the Forest and Raft styles, are essentially triangular. The Broom, which is almost hemispherical, is the only exception.

NEEDLE JUNIPER

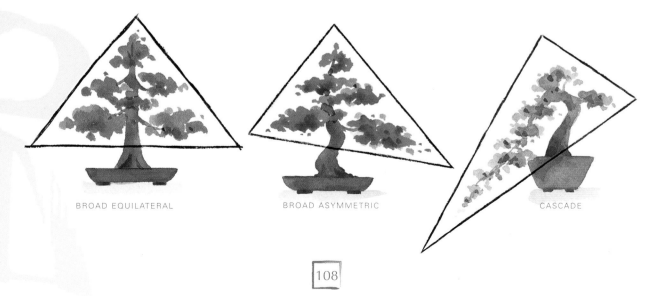

BROAD EQUILATERAL

BROAD ASYMMETRIC

CASCADE

DOES THE TRUNK HAVE TO BE STRAIGHT?

The trunk of a bonsai can be slanting, S-shaped, or curved. The direction in which it leads the eye is what is termed the "movement" of the tree. When you are developing the design of a bonsai, you need to establish this trunk line first. The other details, such as the number and arrangement of the branches, will follow naturally.

OLD COLLECTED CHINESE JUNIPER

TRUNK LINE

The trunk is the second thing you notice about a bonsai after its overall form. It gives the bonsai its character. Bonsai makers always aim to reveal as much of the trunk as possible. If the trunk isn't clearly visible, the bonsai will not be convincing because it will look more like a shrub than a miniature tree.

ROOTS

A bonsai that does not display a set of well-formed roots, or nebari, will lack character. If the bonsai that you are working on does not have clearly visible roots, delve under the soil surface to see if there are any that can be developed. If you don't find any, consider air-layering the lower trunk *(see page 145)* or even grafting new roots onto the trunk *(see page 145).*

SECRETS OF SUCCESS

Look at as many bonsai manuals and magazines as possible to familiarize yourself with examples of well-executed bonsai. Keep these images in mind as models to which you can aspire.

TALL AND THIN TRIANGLE

TALL AND THIN ASYMMETRIC

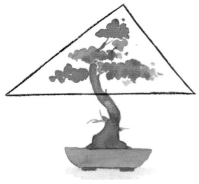

HIGH TRIANGULAR

CHINESE JUNIPER

SPACE

You have only to look at a Japanese Zen garden to realize how important space—or rather "empty space"—is in Eastern design. It is only by creating space that you can appreciate the form, detail, and character of a bonsai. The space between the branches is an obvious example. The space that is created by the clean lines of a Literati tree is another. This driftwood juniper by Masahiko Kimura is asymmetric in design. The space on the left is what gives the tree its unique character.

BRANCHES

A bonsai's branches give it an overall shape, form, and all-important character. The more mature the branches, the older the bonsai will look. Mature branches on deciduous trees are characterized by fine ramification of the twigs, which in winter form a beautiful silhouette.

The placement of the branches along the length of the trunk needn't follow a logical sequence. As long as they are spaced evenly, you will create the right effect. The position of the first branch is ideally a third of the way up the trunk, but there are no hard-and-fast rules.

BRANCH PLACEMENT

Front-facing branches—those on the viewing side—are always better placed at a slight angle, so they do not protrude directly to the front. The first branch on S-shaped, or Informal upright trees, should emerge from the outside elbow of the first bend—seldom from the inside. But as this pine (left) shows, the "rule" can sometimes be broken. Remember, rules should serve only as guidelines—they are not immutable.

BRANCH PAD SIDE ELEVATION

BLACK PINE

BRANCH PAD BIRD'S-EYE VIEW

TOKONAME POTS

POT

The pot can completely alter the appearance of a bonsai, so choosing the right one is critical. As a general rule, the longest dimension, which is usually the length of the pot in the case of shallow pots, should be two-thirds the height of the tree. There are also rules for depth and shape *(see pages 62–63)*. However, never follow convention slavishly. If you use the rules intelligently, without ignoring your instinct for what looks right, you cannot go far wrong.

FOCAL POINT

A good bonsai design is always characterized by some special or outstanding feature. This focal point or center of attraction may be a driftwood effect or a hollow trunk. Whatever it is, it should catch the viewer's imagination and make the bonsai special.

SECRETS OF SUCCESS

When creating a focal point, naturalness must be the overriding concern. Don't be tempted to create a feature that is not suggested by the tree, just for the sake of it. Anything obviously contrived will simply look wrong.

DRIFTWOOD
CHINESE JUNIPER

LITERATI SCOTS PINE

DESIGN ANALYSIS

Bonsai, like painting or sculpture, can be analyzed in terms of line and form, balance and harmony, scale, perspective, color, texture, movement, and overall impression. If you are familiar with these concepts, you will be better able to appreciate why a particular bonsai is superior to another or how you can improve your own bonsai. With practice, good design will become second nature. The best way to develop your expertise is to see as many examples of good bonsai as possible. Working with a good teacher will also take you further.

WABI AND SABI IN BONSAI DESIGN

A knowledge of the Zen origins of bonsai is the key to appreciating the finer points of bonsai design. Zen is central to all Eastern aesthetics, and the concepts of wabi and sabi have a direct relevance to bonsai. Although "wabi-sabi" is often used to denote anything that relates to Japanese design, the two words embody quite distinct spiritual and philosophical values.

In practical terms, wabi and sabi can be seen in seven qualities that are typically Zen. These qualities are: simplicity, tranquillity, naturalness, asymmetry, austere sublimity, freedom from attachment, and subtle profundity. While any one of these qualities may predominate in a bonsai, all should be present to some degree.

1 Simplicity

In Zen philosophy, the most profound thoughts are often expressed in the simplest terms. In bonsai, the most beautiful trees are often those that have the simplest designs. Over-ornate trees or pots detract from the simplicity of elegant design. It can be tempting to get too complicated, but try to be restrained.

2 Tranquillity

One of the most noticeable characteristics of Chinese and Japanese art is the feeling of deep calm, even in the midst of action. Some bonsai are so noble in bearing that they impart a deep sense of restfulness and tranquillity. It is this feeling of tranquillity that makes bonsai so appealing.

The Zen dimension in bonsai is not just about aesthetics: it is an all-embracing visual, intellectual, and spiritual experience.

3 Naturalness

The importance of naturalness in bonsai design cannot be overemphasized. A bad example of a bonsai is one that is so refined that it almost looks plastic. This kind of artificiality should be avoided at all cost. The aim of any bonsai grower is to create an impression of the accidental or incidental, as though this man-made bonsai was, in fact, untouched by a human hand. Observe the characteristics of nature and strive to reproduce these, down to the minutest detail.

4 Asymmetry

Asymmetry, imperfection, and impermanence are inherent characteristics of the Zen approach, whereas Western art implies symmetry, perfection, and permanence. Asymmetry in bonsai does not mean disharmony. Harmony is achieved by a careful balancing of visual mass and empty space in the right places and proportions. The avoidance of opposing, or "bar," branches and the subtle placement of the tree slightly off-center in its pot are typical examples of asymmetrical design.

WHAT ARE WABI AND SABI?

The literal translation of "wabi" is "poverty," but the English does not convey its true meaning. Poverty in this context means not being dependent on material possessions. The poverty of wabi is found in the person who is quietly content with the simple things in life and draws on these for everyday inspiration. Wabi is therefore poverty that surpasses immense riches.

"Sabi" denotes "loneliness" or "solitude," although in aesthetic terms, its meaning is much broader. It implies an antique element, especially if combined with a primitive lack of sophistication. Very old bonsai and antique pots possess this quality. The essence of "sabi," therefore, is gracefulness combined with antiquity.

5 Austere sublimity

The rock and gravel gardens found in Kyoto, Japan, are classic examples of austere sublimity. These gardens often contain no plants at all: only the bare essentials required to convey the message of the artist. Likewise in bonsai, every branch, twist, and bend should fulfill a vital function. The Literati or "Bunjin" (learned scholar) style typifies this quality, where just one or two strong lines communicate the subtleties and emotions of the bonsai artist.

6 Freedom from attachment

This concept is characterized by the freshness that comes from abandoning convention, custom, and formula. In bonsai, it is those trees that break the conventional rules that attract attention because of their original, unorthodox appearance.

7 Subtle profundity

This is perhaps the most difficult concept to convey, involving intimations of inexhaustability and endless reverberations. It carries a suggestion of deep space and some hidden ability or quality. In bonsai, it can be the age of the tree that prompts this feeling, its sheer beauty, or its regal bearing.

This masterpiece embodies everything that bonsai design is all about—freedom from attachment, subtle profundity, austere sublimity, and sheer tranquillity.

BASIC SHAPING TECHNIQUES

The shape of a bonsai can be created by pruning, wiring, or mechanical means. The modern approach is to use all three methods, but in times past, most bonsai were shaped using only cutting tools: mainly pruning knives, scissors, and clippers. Today we have the benefit of sophisticated tools and implements, but they should be regarded only as a means to an end.

CUTTING AND PRUNING

STEP 1

STEP 2

STEP 3

You can create bonsai by simply cutting out unwanted growth and retaining and developing those parts of the tree that are essential to the design. Chinese bonsai growers have been using this method for centuries, and the Lingnan style, still practiced in southern China today, shows what can be achieved by pruning alone. This technique, also known as the "clip and grow" method, relies on channeling the growing points in the direction you want them to go.

The disadvantage of the clip and grow method is that it is slow and the shapes produced tend to be very angular. Precise control of shape is also difficult, because branches tend to grow upward.

Creating horizontal or downward-pointing branches is extremely hard to achieve, so most bonsai practitioners use this technique in conjunction with other methods. Step 1 using the clip-and-grow method would mean cutting at point A. This will encourage shoots to grow at that point. Allow just one to grow in the desired direction—this will form the basis of the next growing point. When this shoot has developed adequately, you can proceed to cut off all the growth at point B. Repeat the process again by cutting at point C to achieve the required change of direction. Once the trunk shape is achieved, the branches can be developed.

TIE ROPES, GUY WIRES, AND WEIGHTS

This method is used when the branches of the tree are too thick to be held in position by wire. It is used extensively for shaping large garden trees such as black pine, five-needle pine, yews, and Japanese holly. Before the introduction of wire, stones and boulders were used as weights to pull down branches into the desired position.

USING WEIGHTS TO BEND BRANCHES

USING GUY WIRES

SHAPING WITH POLES

MECHANICAL AIDS

Bamboo poles have been used for centuries for shaping garden trees and bonsai in China and Japan. It's an efficient method and still in widespread use. The poles serve as a former, or framework, around which the trunk and branches are trained. In good growing conditions, the desired shape can be achieved in just a couple of years. Formers made from metal bars or very heavy-gauge wires are used for creating acute bends or for straightening trunks on Formal upright trees.

SHAPING WITH WIRE

Wire is by far the most effective means of shaping trunks and branches and has the advantage of being neat and elegant. Where intricate detail is needed, such as in the fine ramification of branch pads, wiring is the only method subtle enough to produce the results. Wire is now universally used. Even Chinese bonsai artists who have traditionally relied on shaping by pruning now use wire for achieving the same ends.

WIRE SHAPING ON CHINESE JUNIPER

115

SHAPING TOOLS

You can use many different tools to shape your bonsai. Some are ordinary garden tools, while others are specially designed to carry out a particular bonsai technique. It is not necessary to spend a lot on the latest or most sophisticated tools on the market, but knowing which tool to use for a particular task will ensure that you do the work efficiently and quickly.

 Use general gardening tools to cut large branches and trunks. Specialist bonsai tools will not be as effective, and you will wear out their blades unnecessarily. The rough-cutting tasks are what gives a bonsai its preliminary shape. Once these cuts are made, you can proceed to tidy up the edges using the more precise bonsai tools. Treat the special bonsai tools with care because they are expensive. If a task can be done with gardening tools, use these in preference to the bonsai tools, because they are easier and cheaper to replace.

PRUNERS

 ## PRUNERS

Any roots that cannot be cut easily with bonsai root shears should be cut with pruners or loppers. Both tools are useful for severing the roots of large field-grown trees when they are being lifted from the ground or during repotting. You can also use pruners on branches, if they are no thicker than $\frac{1}{2}$ inch (2 cm). Wear a leather glove on the hand you are not using. Never twist the blades of pruners or loppers while cutting, because it can break the blade.

BRANCH LOPPERS

Loppers are similar to pruners but are larger and have long handles for greater leverage. Use them on thick roots and branches or trunks that are over $\frac{1}{2}$ inch (2 cm) in diameter.

BRANCH LOPPER

SECRETS OF SUCCESS

Always keep tools clean and rust-free because this will keep them in good working order. Clean blades after use with light oil or paintbrush cleaner to remove sap and resin. If you are not going to use a tool for a while, apply grease to the blade to prevent rusting.

JAPANESE SAWS

The principal use of a Japanese saw is to cut those branches that other, less accurate tools cannot tackle. Unlike other saws, which cut on the push stroke, a Japanese saw cuts on the pull stroke. Never use undue force when using one, or you will kink the blade and damage the teeth. You should also avoid using this kind of saw for cutting roots, because the contact with soil particles will damage the delicate blade very quickly.

JAPANESE FOLDING SAW

BOW SAWS

Bow saws are invaluable for cutting large branches, trunks, and roots. They are particularly useful for the preliminary shaping of field-grown material where precision and accuracy are not needed.

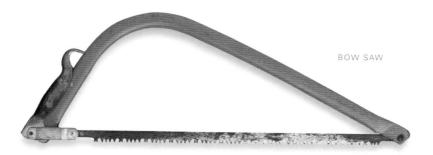

BOW SAW

TOOL CARE

- Always clean tools after use.

- Apply a light oil to the cutting blades after cleaning, or grease if the tool will not be used for a while.

- Keep tools sharp by using a whetstone or diamond sharpener.

- Mark your tools with tape or paint so that they don't get mixed up with other people's tools when you attend workshops or classes.

- Try to avoid dropping cutting tools such as scissors and branch cutters on stone or concrete floors—this will damage the tips of the blades.

- Store tools safely in a toolbox or tool roll.

- Don't carry tools in your hand luggage when traveling by air. They should be checked with your main baggage.

117

SPECIALIST BONSAI CUTTERS

These tools are specially designed for bonsai growers and perform the tasks that general gardening tools cannot tackle. All specialist bonsai tools are made in both black steel and stainless steel. The stainless steel versions are considerably more expensive but are more economical in the long run, because they don't rust and they stay sharp for much longer.

THE BRANCH SPLITTER

Known in Japan as the branch "cracker," this specialist tool is used for splicing relatively thick branches to facilitate bending. The branch is split into two or more longitudinal sections so that they form a laminate of two or more thinner pieces of wood that are much easier to bend into the desired shape. When using the tool, let the blades meet but do not bend or twist the tool because this can break the blade tips.

BEGIN AT BASE

CONTINUE ALONG THE TRUNK

THE ROOT CUTTER

You can use a root cutter if you do not have a branch splitter. It is very similar in shape. Its main use is for cutting thick roots during repotting. It can also be used to cut away any protruding surface roots and thereby improve a bonsai's nebari. Most of the Japanese bonsai tools cut cleanly and close to the surface. Unlike ordinary pruners, they do not leave stubby ends. The root cutter can also serve as a concave branch cutter.

WHICH BONSAI TOOLS ARE ESSENTIAL?

You can accomplish almost anything in bonsai using these five tools. Other tools are useful but not essential, and you can always improvise.

- pruners
- concave branch cutter
- long-handle twig shears
- root pruning shears
- root rake

If you have more money to spend, then consider:

- wen (or full concave) cutter
- hybrid cutter
- bonsai wire cutter
- branch splitter
- root cutter
- leaf or twig shears
- heavy-duty root hook
- set of soil sieves

NIBBLING AT ROOTS

BRANCH CUTTERS

There are three main designs of branch cutter: the "flat concave," the "wen" or "full concave," and the "hybrid" cutter. Each can be used to cut branches flush to the trunk without leaving a stub.

The flat concave cutter does the job of ordinary garden pruners, only with much greater precision. Keep it to use exclusively for trimming branches close to the trunk and don't be tempted to use it as a general pruning tool. When you wish to remove a branch, use the pruners first to make a rough cut and then use the flat concave cutter to finish off the cut as flush to the trunk as possible. The wen cutter has a fully concave or spherical cutting blade. It is used to cut into the trunk to create a shallow concave depression. The cut is then covered with wound sealant or cut paste and forms a completely smooth surface when the bark heals over.

The spherical shaped blades of the wen cutter are not designed for use as a general branch pruning tool. The flat concave branch cutter fulfills that role.

The hybrid cutter is a versatile tool, introduced by Japanese toolmakers to combine the functions of the flat branch cutter and the wen cutter. You may choose to invest in one of these rather than buying two separate tools.

Always try to handle a tool before you buy so you can get a feel of what it is like to use.

CUTTING WITH HYBRID CUTTER

CORRECT USE OF BRANCH CUTTER

CONCAVE CUT WITH HYBRID CUTTER

WRONG USE OF BRANCH CUTTER

WRONG USE OF WEN CUTTER

CORRECT USE OF WEN CUTTER

119

SPECIALIST BONSAI SCISSORS

There are many bonsai scissors available, each with a specific use. Some have large handles, others small handles; some have long blades, while others have short blades. Left-handed bonsai growers can also buy specialist scissors. Bonsai scissors can be divided into three general groups, each serving one of three main purposes: cutting roots, cutting twigs, and cutting leaves.

Large-handle scissors are the most convenient scissors you can use to cut roots. The large handles allow a good grip, and the long blades shear through a mass of roots easily.

Long-handle scissors are used to cut twigs. The long handle makes it easy to penetrate the twig structure and pick out precisely what you want to prune.

LONG-HANDLE SCISSORS   LARGE-HANDLE SCISSORS

LEAF PRUNER

LEAF PRUNERS

These are particularly handy for defoliating or leaf-cutting your bonsai. Trees that have dense foliage, such as the Kiyohime and Kashima maples, are leaf pruned in summer. This tool makes light work of leaf-cutting because the spring-loaded action enables you to work fast. If you had to use scissors for this operation, it would take twice as long, or even more!

WIRE CUTTERS AND PLIERS

These specialist tools have an ease of use that makes them ideal for intricate work—they differ greatly from conventional gardening wire cutters and pliers. There are a number of different designs of wire cutter: some resemble pliers, while others are more like snub-nosed scissors. The latter are particularly useful for snipping thin wires. Jin pliers are used mainly to strip off bark when making jins.

ORDINARY PLIERS

JIN PLIERS

JIN PLIERS

120

CHISELS AND GRAFTING KNIVES

Carving tools are extremely useful for creating driftwood effects. Ordinary carpentry chisels are perfectly adequate, but the Japanese bonsai chisels are specially designed to create the jins and sharis used in bonsai.

Japanese grafting knives have a number of different uses, including grafting, removing the flaking bark off juniper trees, and jinning. Although the modern trend is to use power tools for carving, conventional hand tools are still preferred by many masters.

CHISELS AND GRAFTING KNIVES

POWER TOOLS

Electric power tools are now used extensively in bonsai, mainly for creating driftwood effects. Most are ordinary power tools adapted for bonsai work with specialist cutting bits.

The power tools most often used are the industrial die grinder and angle grinder, rotary cutters such as the high-speed router, rotary and reciprocating saws, and rotary hobby carvers for fine work. Chain saws can also be used to cut thick branches or trunks, but they should never be used as a carving tool.

SAFETY

- **Always wear appropriate protective gear before using a cutting tool, such as a helmet, face shield, dust mask, goggles, and gloves.**

- **Keep a first-aid kit in case of accidents.**

- **If possible, do your cutting work when someone else is around, in case you need help in an emergency.**

- **Check that electrical tools are safe before use by ensuring that there are no loose or exposed cable ends or frayed insulation. Use an earth leakage circuit breaker or trip device to isolate the electrical appliance in case of an electrical fault.**

- **Before using a cutting tool, look around you and assess the hazards of the situation.**

- **Make sure the cutting bits are sharp and firmly attached to the chuck. Blunt tools are inefficient and dangerous. Cutting bits that are not fastened securely may fly off and cause serious injury.**

ROTARY CUTTER

7

SHAPING
TECHNIQUES

*"Creating bonsai is not a mechanistic process;
we prune with the hand but are guided by the heart."*

WIRING

When bonsai was in its infancy in Europe in the 1960s and 1970s, specialist bonsai wire was very difficult to obtain. Most enthusiasts improvised by using the wire from coat hangers and overhead electric cables. Today specialist bonsai wire is widely available at all bonsai outlets—the three most common types of bonsai wire are aluminum, annealed copper, and iron.

Wire is the singlemost important accessory in bonsai—with the use of wire, a tree can be transformed almost instantly from a plain shrub to an exquisite work of art. All the images that a bonsai artist has in his or her mind cannot be realized unless the tree is transformed into tangible shapes by using wire.

Once the wire is applied, it is simply a matter of time for the desired shape to be achieved. Perhaps the most important skill in the art of bonsai is good wiring technique. Many people have either never been taught how to wire properly or take short cuts with their wiring. A good grounding in wiring is therefore a prerequisite to progressing further in bonsai. In Japan, bonsai apprentices take a couple of years to become proficient in wiring. An amateur would need almost a lifetime to achieve the same standard. Remember that wiring is only a means to an end—the ultimate object being to achieve the desired shape in a bonsai.

HOW TO WIRE

  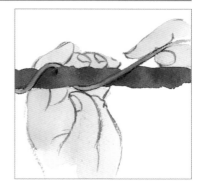

❶ Apply the wire with a winding action, clockwise or counterclockwise. Apply the wire fairly tightly. You should not be able to see daylight between the bark and the wire, but do not wire so tightly as to cut into the bark.

❷ Grip the branch and the wire with one hand as you wind the wire around the branch with the other. Pull the wire taut with the thumb and forefinger of one hand and grip the coil that has just been completed with the other as you move along.

❸ Move your hand along as each coil is applied, keeping both hands close together at all times. Space each coil evenly around the branch at a 45-degree angle. Do not space the coils too closely or too widely apart *(see page 128 for examples)*.

TYPES OF WIRE

IRON

Iron wire is the most often used by commercial bonsai nurseries because it the cheapest wire available. Most of the indoor trees that originate from China are also shaped with iron wire. Although effective, it is stiff and hard to bend, which makes it difficult to use as well as also to remove from a bonsai once it has been put on. Iron wire can also rust, which looks unsightly. It is best to avoid using iron wire since copper and aluminum wire is now widely available.

COPPER

Copper wire is also stiff, but when annealed, or tempered by heat treatment, it becomes as pliable and easy to use as aluminum. You can use it in this state to apply to a tree and leave it to harden. It will keep its hardened shape permanently, which greatly reduces the risk of a wired branch being accidentally knocked out of shape. Copper wire—which is far more expensive than aluminum—is used when the grower needs the wiring to stay in place for several years, as in the case of coniferous trees. It is not often used on deciduous trees, because it can damage and mark their soft bark.

ALUMINUM

Aluminum is soft and pliable, which makes it extremely easy to handle. It can also be recycled and used again. When produced for bonsai use, it is normally anodized brown so that it blends with the trunk or branch, although clear aluminum wire is also widely used. Some bonsai professionals prefer the clear wire, because it is highly visible and makes it unlikely they'll forget to remove it at the appropriate time, before it marks the bark. Clear wire also reflects heat better and, in hot sunshine, is therefore not as harsh on the bark as dark wire.

Aluminum is used mainly on deciduous trees because the wiring is short term—usually three to six months—and therefore strength over time is not so important. Most of the wiring on deciduous trees involves only the very young, flexible branches. The thicker branches are more liable to break if you try bending them. The wiring is also comparatively loose; the aim is to point the branch in the right direction rather than create the intricate bends, cranks, and curves that are associated with coniferous trees. Only the first- and second-year shoots of deciduous trees need to be wired, because most deciduous trees look more natural with minimal pruning and light wiring.

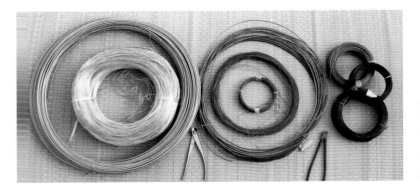

On the left, the outer coil is iron wire, the inner coil is clear aluminum wire. In the center is annealed copper wire; on the right is brown anodized aluminum wire.

WIRING BRANCHES: TWO-BRANCHES PRINCIPLE

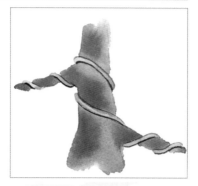

1 Wiring is most effective if it is anchored to something. It may be the trunk, a branch, or a piece of "jin." The neatest solution is another branch adjacent to the one you are wiring (to avoid wrapping it around the trunk). One branch will therefore serve as the anchor point for the other.

2 If the adjacent branch you wish to use as an anchor is some distance away from the one you are wiring, then simply go around the main trunk with a full or half coil and then latch on to the other branch, as shown above. Remember to keep the wire taut at all times.

3 When done properly, the wire should look like this—neat and tidy. This is what we refer to as the two-branch principle. One branch acts as the anchor for the other and vice versa. There is no need to have ugly wire ends wrapped around the trunk for anchorage.

4 Where branches are at the same level or directly opposite each other (sometimes referred to as "bar" or handlebar branches), you do not need to coil the wire around the trunk. Just take the wire straight across from one branch to the other.

WHEN SHOULD A TREE BE REWIRED?

It is not just young trees that have to be wired; even old-specimen trees need restyling and rewiring from time to time. When a tree has lost its shape, that is the time to rewire.

This Chinese juniper has been pruned and thinned out before the branches were wired. The wiring has been done to create this carefully designed triangular shape.

126

WIRING A TRUNK

❶ If a trunk is pliable enough and can be bent into shape, wiring can be used to achieve this end. Insert the wire into the soil to anchor it in position.

❷ Wrap the wire around the trunk and take it right up to the apex of the tree. If one coil is insufficient to bend the trunk, try using a double coil of wire instead. Remember, always wire the trunk before the branches.

COPPER WIRE

Copper wire, which will keep its shape over a long period, is traditionally used on coniferous bonsai. Also, it is harder than aluminum, so it is possible to match the strength of an aluminum wire with much thinner copper wire. Copper also turns darker over time, which makes it more discreet if the conifer is exhibited.

WIRING WITHOUT CROSSING WIRES

❶ When wiring the trunk or the branches, you will find branches of different thicknesses. If these branches are to be wired, they will require wire of different thicknesses. Always wire the thickest stem first, using the appropriate grade of wire.

❷ Proceed to the next thickest stem, with a slightly thinner grade of wire. Remember to use the two-branch principle; that is, linking two adjacent branches with one piece of wire.

❸ Next, go on to the slightly thinner stems or branches using even thinner wire. Do not cross the wires at any stage—they should flow in the same direction. Wire the foliage pads in a flat plane and preferably in a triangular herringbone pattern.

EXAMPLES OF GOOD WIRING

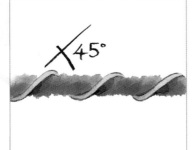

EVEN SPACING

Wiring should look good and be neat and tidy. The ideal way to wire is to maintain an even spacing. This is best achieved by winding the wire at a 45-degree angle and applying it fairly tightly.

DOUBLE STRANDING

If a single coil of wire will not hold the branch in place, try a thicker gauge of wire. If this does not work, consider using a double strand—it is important to follow the same path and avoid crossing wires.

EXAMPLES OF POOR WIRING

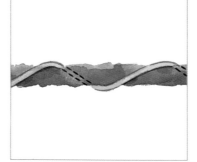

TOO CLOSE

If the coils of wire are too close together, it will act like a spring and be less effective. Wiring too closely is also wasteful and untidy in appearance.

TOO FAR APART

Wiring too far apart is also ineffective because the wire will not be able to hold the branch or trunk in place. Being too widely spaced, the wire cannot hold acute bends. The angle here is not the ideal 45 degrees.

HOW LONG SHOULD WIRE BE LEFT ON?

Young shoots that have been wired should take only one growing season to set. If the shoot or branch is slightly older and thicker, it may take two or more years to set. The only way to tell is to remove the wire and see if the branch has taken the intended shape. If the branch springs back, wire the branch again.

SATZUKI AZALEAS

Although evergreen, Satsuki azaleas are wired with aluminum, because only their thin shoots and branches are wired. The thick branches would break if any attempt was made to wire them.

TIPS FOR
GOOD WIRING

- Use the correct gauge of wire. If it is too thin, it will not do the job; if it is too thick, it could damage or break the branch.

- Wire the trunk first (if applicable) and then the branches.

- Wire from the bottom up, and work toward the crown.

- Always use one piece of wire for two adjacent branches—the two-branch principle.

- A double wire of a slightly thinner gauge is more effective than a single thick wire.

- Wire at a 45-degree angle—the coils should neither be too closely or too widely spaced because this will make the wiring less effective.

- Wire fairly tightly, but not overtight. You can usually tell if the wire is too tight if it bites into the bark. If the wire is too loose, it may grate the bark when you bend the branch.

- Hold the branch in one hand, and use the other hand to coil the wire around the branch. Proceed outward.

- Remove wire from the tree as soon as it starts to "bite," to avoid wire marks.

- If the wire is difficult to remove by uncoiling, use wire cutters.

- Fall and winter, when growth is not active, are good times for wiring.

- You can practice your wiring technique on a piece of plastic tubing or a bamboo cane. Try using aluminum first and then copper. The two materials are quite different.

A BEGINNER'S GUIDE
TO SHAPING BONSAI

- Use clean, sharp tools.

- Use appropriate tools—don't try to cut a thick trunk with shears or scissors.

- Think twice before you cut, because you can only cut once.

- Choose a tree that has a lot of branches.

- Choose a tree that has an interesting trunk—the more gnarled the better.

- Explore every angle before deciding which side will become the front of your tree—or it may be easier to identify an obvious back.

- Identify the trunk line *(see page 109)*—once you establish this, the rest will follow naturally.

- Establish the first branch—usually the first major low branch.

- Establish the overall triangular shape.

- Make sure you have all the grades of wire that you need.

- Wire the trunk into shape—if you wish to bend the trunk.

- Try to establish a good taper to the apex.

- Wire the branches next, starting with the lowest branch and working upward.

- Choose the thin branches for your design rather than the thick ones—the thin branches will be more in scale with the rest of the tree.

- Put your tree into a temporary or final pot, depending on the season. Never put your tree into a pot before shaping and wiring, because you may change your mind about which is the front of the tree as you work.

CREATING JINS AND SHARIS

Jins and sharis are the driftwood features used extensively in contemporary bonsai. "Jin" is the dead wood on the tip of a branch or on the apex of a tree. "Shari" is the exposed part of the main trunk, which has been stripped of its bark. These features are often the result of storm damage. When a branch is ripped from a trunk, the stub is bleached to a beautiful silvery color.

 In bonsai, you can imitate the effects of storm damage by carefully tearing off a branch and stripping the bark from the trunk. To add to the effect and make it look as natural as possible, you can then carve the exposed dead wood.

Jins and sharis should look as natural as possible in order to be convincing. If they look too contrived, they will not enhance the bonsai. It is only by practicing that you will improve your technique. To begin, practice on discarded branches rather than on live bonsai.

MAKING JINS

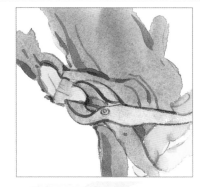

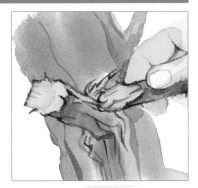

① A good way of initiating a jin is to make a sloping cut using a concave branch cutter—not the wen cutter. Cut at an angle, pointing away from the trunk or branch, and cut a third or halfway into the wood. This will now enable you to initiate the break.

② The next step is to snap or break the branch at the point where the cut has been made. Snap the branch off and pull it toward the trunk. The tearing action should expose the natural grain of the wood, giving it a rough texture.

③ Pull the wood right back to where the branch starts so that as much of the grain as possible is exposed. If you like, you can pull away more slivers of wood using a pair of jin pliers so that more grain is exposed.

MAKING JINS—ALTERNATIVE METHOD

1 An alternative method of making jins, especially on thicker branches of 1 inch (2.5 cm) or more in diameter, is to use the "quartering" technique. Select a branch that you wish to jin. Keep the jins short— excessively long jins look unnatural. Saw off the branch with a sharp saw.

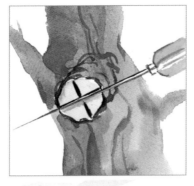

2 Using the saw—cut partly into the exposed surface, making a cross-cut pattern. Cut about 1 inch (2.5 cm) into the stump—or deeper for a longer jin. The resulting quadrants will facilitate jinning because each quadrant will be easier to strip than a solid, thick piece of wood.

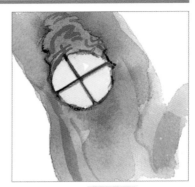

3 Done correctly—this is what it should look like. Check that the wood is sound and not rotten. If the branch that you cut was a live one, there should be no problem. If the branch was dead, the wood might not be sound.

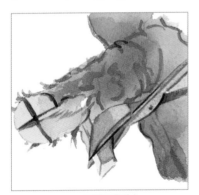

4 Using a flat, concave branch cutter, grip each quadrant in turn and tear off the pieces by peeling back the wood as far as it will go. Do this to all four quadrants so that a roughly conical shape is achieved.

5 When peeling the wood back, do a little at a time. Don't try to rip off huge chunks of wood, because this could spoil the jin and you also risk breaking the blade of your branch cutter.

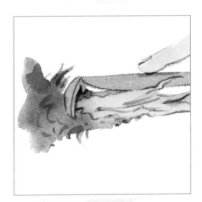

6 Using a sickle-shaped jinning tool, scrape off all the remaining bark from the jinned stub. You might find a penknife or box cutter equally effective. Don't use the tool to remove any wood because this will spoil the natural texture achieved by the tearing action.

MAKING JINS—ALTERNATIVE METHOD

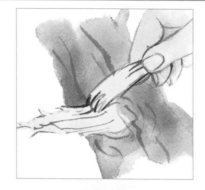

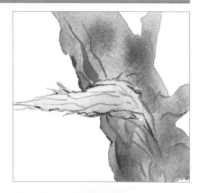

7 You can refine the jin by tearing away slivers of wood with a pair of long-nose pliers. Keep tearing at the wood until the desired shape and texture of the jin have been achieved. Don't be disappointed if you cannot create a good jin on your first attempt. Everything requires practice.

8 If you wish to reduce the jin farther, do it carefully by tearing slivers of wood by hand. It is important to show the natural torn texture rather than a surface that has been whittled away using a knife.

9 When you are satisfied with the shape and texture of the jin, you can then remove any burrs and loose debris with a small blowtorch or sandpaper. A blowtorch is useful because it leaves faint burn marks—these blend in well with the lime sulfur that will be applied next.

10 Lime sulfur is applied directly to the bare wood using a soft brush. Newly created jins should be allowed to dry out thoroughly for at least a month before applying lime sulfur. Never apply lime sulfur in the strong sunshine, because it will turn yellow. Do it in the shade.

The greatest exponent of jins and sharis is Masahiko Kimura. This massive *Taxus cuspidata* is one of his masterpieces.

MAKING SHARIS

1 Mark the area that you wish to turn into shari or driftwood trunk, using a thick felt-tip marker to draw the outline. Make the outline as natural looking as possible by using curved lines rather than straight lines. Hatch the area that is to be stripped of its bark.

2 Once the shari area has been finalized, you can start to remove the bark by cutting with a knife or chisel. Follow the outline that you have marked very carefully, making sure not to deviate from the original plan.

3 When all the bark has been removed, you can proceed to cut into the wood using a knife or a chisel. If you feel competent to use a power tool such as a die-grinder, this may do the job more quickly.

TEARING
Sometimes a shari can be created by tearing off the bark and wood, as shown here. The tearing action will leave a very natural texture that no other means can create.

This massive Chinese juniper was in the author's collection for many years. The shari is natural, but much of the detail has been enhanced by carving with precision power tools.

RESTYLING AND GROOMING

To stay looking their best, bonsai require regular pruning, refining, grooming, and occasional restyling. Without care of this kind, a bonsai will soon start to deteriorate physically and aesthetically. The principles of restyling and grooming bonsai are similar to what we do with our hair. Unless our hair is cared for properly, it will soon become unkempt and disheveled.

 The following examples illustrate how grooming and restyling principles should be applied to trees that have become overgrown, have developed a major defect, or have simply lost their way.

Restyling and grooming are about restoring bonsai to their former glory or, in some cases, turning ordinary bonsai into spectacular specimens.

The principles are the same as those we apply to styling and creating bonsai from scratch:
(a) study the tree for its potential;
(b) determine which is the best viewing side, for example, the "front" of the tree;
(c) decide what needs to be done to the various parts to improve its look—the roots, trunk, branches, and apex;

This twin-trunk mountain maple has been neglected for many years by its owner. As a result, the branches have become too dense and unstructured.

With a bit of radical pruning and restructuring of the branches, the tree now looks more refined and elegant. A larger oval pot suits the tree better.

The same tree a couple of months later. Note the light, airy feeling that the tree now has. Its elegance has been restored.

This large mountain maple has been in the author's collection for over 30 years. It is a very old tree, but has become too overgrown and straggly in recent years. The branches are excessively long, making the crown too large for its trunk. The tree is well over 4 feet (1.3 m) high, and the whole proportion between crown and trunk looks unbalanced.

In the spring, it was decided to prune the tree quite radically in order to make it more compact. This is what the tree looked like immediately after pruning.

(d) consider the best planting angle;
(e) consider whether the pot suits the tree.

   Good-quality trees, or "specimens" as they are referred to by enthusiasts, do not often require radical restructuring, although this is what the great bonsai artist Kimura does to many famous bonsai in Japan. As a rule, they just need to be lightly pruned or refined, rewired, and perhaps planted in a new pot.

During the following summer, the new shoots were allowed to grow to three or four nodes and were then pruned back to the first node to induce more ramification, or twigginess. This is what the tree looked like by late summer. It is much more compact now, and the early fall color is just beginning to show on the leaves.

Grooming a juniper

Chinese junipers make extremely fine bonsai. They are now one of the most sought after species in Europe and North America. Although generally hardy, they can be temperamental if the soil conditions and watering regime are not quite right. When grown well, they are so vigorous that they will become overgrown very easily. On the other hand, if the growing conditions are not ideal, they will gradually deteriorate.

This Chinese juniper has been in the author's collection for almost 30 years. It was in a very poor condition to begin with, but by careful nurturing in sphagnum moss and a very open soil mix, the tree finally recovered and it now displays very lush green growth throughout the year.

The juniper before grooming is healthy and vigorous, but its vigor will cause the tree to become overgrown and unkempt unless it is groomed at regular intervals.

1 This juniper is extremely healthy, but it is no longer elegant, because it is much too dense. In its present condition, it cannot be exhibited. It was planted in this deep pot to improve drainage and to stabilize the tree.

2 The first step is to thin out the foliage on all the branch pads. This is done with the long-handle twig shears, because it is very easy to penetrate the dense structure with this tool. It is best to start from the bottom and work your way to the top.

GROOMING EVERGREENS

Thin out the foliage pads so that you are able to see the spaces between the branches. Use copper wire because it holds the shape better over a longer period. By keeping the growing tips pinched, the tree will remain in good condition for at least a couple of years. After that, it will have to be regroomed.

3 Take care to prune uniformly so that no section is left either too sparse or too dense. When the entire tree has been pruned, this is what it should look like. It seems a shame to remove all the lovely foliage, but it has to be done if the tree is to look elegant.

4 The branches that have been thinned out are now ready for wiring. This is what it should look like—not very inspiring at the moment, but once the twigs have been wired, they will look quite different.

5 This is a very old tree with an estimated age of over 100 years. The jins and sharis are all natural, but they need to be cleaned and spruced up to look their best. The bark is deflaked using a fine chisel, and the live vine is cleaned using a brass wire brush.

The juniper restored to its former glory. The foliage pads have been thinned out so that each layer is clearly defined and visible. The tree now looks elegant and no longer resembles a tangled mass of foliage.

6 The tree has now been pruned and tidied up, but the wiring has yet to be done. Until the twigs are wired, they will hang limp and look a little disheveled. Wiring will soon set the twigs into the right position, and the foliage pads will look resplendent.

LEAF PRUNING

Leaf pruning, or defoliation, involves removing some or all of the foliage from a tree. It is carried out on deciduous trees during the summer in order to stimulate the production of a second leaf crop. Leaf pruning is done for quite specific reasons, as will be explained below. It shouldn't be done just for the sake of doing it.

Leaf pruning is not done solely to reduce the size of the leaves. As well as helping to produce new leaves and twigs in order to improve branch ramification, there are many other advantages to leaf pruning. Pruning helps to let more light into a dense twig structure and prevents die-back of twigs. It helps to control the vigor of branches and, in some cases, can reduce the size of the leaves. Better fall color is also the result of effective pruning. If you want to transplant a deciduous tree in summer, leaf-prune it first. Because the roots do not have to supply any leaves with water, they can use their energy to reestablish themselves in their new soil.

CUTTING

LEAF PRUNING
Leaf pruning can be done either with long-handle twig shears or with the spring-loaded leaf pruners. Cut off the leaf, leaving the petiole.

This large trident maple was leaf-pruned just a month ago. Because the tree has been exposed to full sun, a new crop of leaves has grown.

LEAF-PRUNING TIPS

- After leaf pruning, water in moderation until the new leaves emerge. Check that the soil is just damp and not soaking wet. Excessive watering will rot the tree's roots.

- Don't fertilize immediately after leaf pruning, because leaves are needed to convert the nutrients into the starches needed for the tree's growth.

- Leaf-prune in early to midsummer, when the leaves have hardened. Don't leaf-prune after midsummer, because the new leaves need time to mature before they fall.

- New leaves normally take between four to six weeks to emerge after defoliation.

- Defoliated trees can be left in full sun, but do not let new leaves burn. You can prevent this by ensuring that the soil does not dry out completely—it should be damp, not soggy.

- To strengthen a weak branch, leaf-prune the whole tree except that particular branch.

- To reduce the vigor of a strong branch, defoliate just that branch and leave all the other branches untouched.

- If you forget to water a deciduous bonsai on a hot day and the leaves shrivel, defoliate all the dried leaves. If you keep the root ball just damp, not wet and soggy, the tree will leaf out again within three to four weeks.

SMALL LEAF MAPLES

Small-leaf maples such as "Kiyohime" and "Kashima" (Yatsabusa or dwarf maples), are leaf-pruned to allow light into their dense twig structure. Without leaf pruning, many of the twigs inside the tree would die. Leaf pruning is most effective when carried out on maples and other deciduous species that have large leaves, such as horse chestnut and sycamore. Never leaf-prune conifers or other evergreens, including Satsuki azaleas and fruiting trees.

SECRETS OF SUCCESS

Leaf pruning puts a tree under stress because it forces it to leaf twice in one season. There is always a risk that it could die, so it shouldn't be carried out routinely. Never defoliate a weak tree.

Leave the petioles remaining on the twigs. After a few weeks, they will fall off just before the new leaves emerge.

The new leaves normally take between four and six weeks to emerge. The new leaves on this trident maple are a lovely bronze color.

8

ADVANCED TECHNIQUES

"Bonsai creation is an unending quest for artistic perfection."

CREATING GOOD TAPER ON BONSAI

The term "taper" in bonsai refers to the gradual tapering of the trunk as it rises from the soil surface to the apex of the tree. A high-quality bonsai is one that has a good taper. The trunk should not appear abruptly chopped at the apex, because this would make the tree look unnatural and ugly. An immature or poor-quality bonsai usually has a truncated apex.

 Most bonsai are made by reducing the height of ordinary trees and regrowing the apex or leader so that the scale of the bonsai is in keeping with the traditional image we have of a bonsai. Invariably, the thicker the trunk, the older the tree appears. But trunk thickness on its own is no substitute for grace and beauty. A beautiful trunk has movement and character. These qualities usually come from having a good taper; that is, one that gradually narrows as it grows upward.

Taper is produced by repeated cutting of the leader in order to produce a new shoot which will be thinner than the preceding one. The process is like building a pyramid: each successive tier or layer is thinner than the previous one. Over a period of

time, the trunk will taper to a narrow point. A great deal of time and patience is required when it comes to creating taper. It is a demanding discipline but very rewarding in what it can teach the bonsai aspirant about attaining perfection.

Although examples of good taper are most noticeable in deciduous trees, especially in winter when the leaves have fallen, evergreen subjects are not exempt from this important requirement. All bonsai, whatever the species, must have good taper if they are to look natural and convincing.

There are some shortcuts. Growing bonsai in large containers or in the open ground can speed up the process considerably, although a period of 10 to 20 years is still about average for achieving success. Fast-growing subjects such as trident maple and hornbeam are favorites for developing good taper because they are very obliging in producing vigorous shoots in the desired locations on the trunk. It is possible to achieve good taper with other species, too. Experiment with different varieties and see how they respond to various growing programs. As you progress in bonsai, much of the pleasure is in trying new techniques.

An example of good taper on a trident maple. Imperfections are easy to hide when a tree is in full leaf, but an expert can tell a good tree from a bad one.

GOOD TAPERING

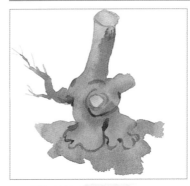

① This large heavy tree trunk had been growing in the ground for the past five years. Its girth is due largely to the free growing conditions in the open ground. To create a nice taper, the existing apex is cut off so the tree will grow a new leader in spring or early summer.

② In the spring, new shoots will sprout from all over the trunk. The shoot chosen for the new leader is the one growing toward the front. Cut off the other shoots so this one will grow vigorously and eventually merge with the existing trunk in a gradual taper.

③ Over the next two years, the new leader is allowed to grow unhampered so that it thickens rapidly. Then the tall leader will be cut off, and the whole process will begin again. By repeatedly cutting the new leader, a gradual reduction of the taper will result.

Creating a good taper takes time: like a good wine—it cannot be hurried.

④ Over a period of 10 to 20 years a perfect taper will emerge. At this stage the branches and fine ramification can be developed.

TRUNK, ROOTS, AND BRANCHES

In bonsai, perfection is something that one is striving for at every stage of a tree's development. A perfect specimen doesn't just happen. It has to be created. Over the years, bonsai growers have devised many techniques for improving various parts of a tree's anatomy. These secrets have only recently been made more widely known to the amateur fraternity.

 The aesthetic features of a bonsai are its trunk, surface roots, and branches. Fortunately, improving these features is not as difficult as you might imagine. Trunks, roots, and branches can be dramatically transformed by applying simple "cosmetic surgery" such as grafting, plaiting, and wiring. There are many different techniques that the professionals use. What follows are just some of the more popular methods. Where branches are defective, in-arch grafting of branches from the same tree can be used to create additional ones. Approach grafting, using branches from another tree, is also effective. The same techniques may be used for creating better surface roots, too.

GRAFTING BRANCHES BY IN-ARCHING

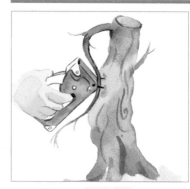

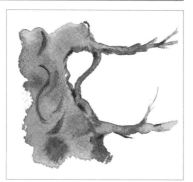

① Select a long, pliable shoot that is no more than a couple of years old. In-arch it onto the trunk and staple it in position using an ordinary stapler. Leave it in place, and in a year's time it should have grafted itself onto the trunk.

② Nothing should be done to restrict the growth of the in-arched branch, since the object is to encourage the grafted branch to thicken as much as possible.

③ When the grafted branch has developed sufficiently, it can be severed from the source and allowed to grow independently.

TRUNK THICKENING

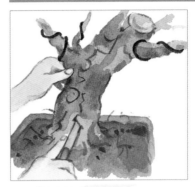

① A thin trunk can be thickened considerably by cutting vertical slits in its bark using a box-cutter or penknife. If the cuts are made jagged rather than straight, the end result will appear natural instead of looking artificial.

② When the bark ages, the slits will blend in with the natural crusty texture of the trunk itself, particularly on pine trunks. When the bottom of a trunk is thinner than the upper portion (inverse taper), it can be rectified using this method.

WIRE METHOD
Leaving wire permanently embedded in the trunk will make the trunk swell. This is a tried-and-tested method of thickening trunks and is especially popular with pine bonsai growers in southern Japan.

An easy way of improving surface roots is to graft young cuttings or seedlings onto the trunk of a defective tree. As the stems of the young donor plants thicken, they will look like genuine old roots of the recipient tree.

Air layering is a useful means of improving surface roots where roots are defective or nonexistent. Very often, a bonsai may have good roots on one side but not on the other—air layering the defective side will correct the problem.

The "plate root" or "turtle back" effect can be developed by growing the tree in shallow, restricted pots. Some growers place tiles or flat pieces of rock under the roots while the trees are grown in the open ground to achieve this effect.

FIELD-GROWING TECHNIQUES

The impressively large bonsai that you see at exhibitions and bonsai shows are often only 20 or 30 years old. These bonsai begin life as field-planted trees that, once allowed to thicken for a few years, are dug up and trained into bonsai. To grow your own mature-looking trees and cut down on years of waiting, all you need is space in your flower bed or vegetable patch.

 Young seedlings and cuttings develop at a much faster rate in the open ground than in pots or containers. Field growing allows the young plants to grow unchecked until the trunks attain the desired thickness. Then they are dug up and trained as bonsai.

Since most bonsai need to have reasonably thick trunks to look mature, most bonsai nurserymen use the open-ground technique to produce the raw material for bonsai in as short a time as possible. It is not just mass-produced bonsai that start off life this way; many high-quality specimens spend their initial years in the growing fields. There is no stigma to developing bonsai this way. In fact, it makes good sense, because it saves years of valuable growing time.

Most bonsai enthusiasts who do not have a lot of room in their gardens simply make do with growing their trees in a flower bed, vegetable patch, or in large wooden boxes. However, a little patience is needed because you will need to leave the tree in the ground for at least two to three years to have the desired effect. A year in the ground is not long enough.

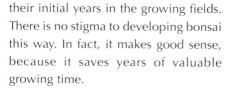

This tree is well on the way to becoming a good-specimen bonsai. The main branches have been selected, and they will be allowed to grow freely during the coming season in order to thicken the trunk and encourage a good taper.

FIELD-GROWING TIPS

- Young trees need space to grow. Plant them 2–3 feet (60–90 cm) apart.

- Once planted, do not disturb your young tree for at least two years. Let the roots and shoots grow naturally.

- Do not attempt to shape a tree's branches and twigs while it is growing in the ground. Wait until it has been transplanted into a pot.

- Feed the tree regularly, using a high N feed in the spring and a low N but high P and K feed in late summer. Use a small quantity of fertilizer once a month from spring until about August or September.

- Once the trunk of the tree is as thick as you want it, start to develop the taper. Cut the apex of the tree, then let it grow, and then cut again, until you achieve the desired result.

- When you lift the tree from the ground in early spring, plant it in a box or shallow pot. Remove the field soil as directed below, taking care not to break fine feeder roots. If it is a deciduous tree, remove up to three-quarters of the field soil. If the tree is an evergreen, remove no more than half.

- Plant the newly lifted tree in a mixture of sand and Akadama, or clay granules, and keep it in an unheated greenhouse or plastic tunnel. Keep away from frost and drafts. Once the new leaves have emerged, put the tree outside, provided there is no risk of frost.

- Remove branches that are too thick. Keep only those that are in scale with the rest of the tree.

When planted in the ground, trees develop at a much faster rate and consequently, thicken more rapidly. Young trees and saplings can quadruple in size in fewer than four years.

SECRET OF SUCCESS

To develop a thick trunk, let the tree grow in the ground for at least five years. In the fourth spring, lift the tree and trim thick roots. Replant. This encourages the fine roots that eventually make good nebari.

ROCK PLANTING WITH THREE JUNIPERS

The Chinese influence on bonsai is all-pervasive because the art originated there. Many of the traditions, techniques, and styles used today have their roots in Chinese culture. The creation of living landscapes using miniature trees and rocks is one such example. Bonsai is about creating a picture—that is why the Chinese call this "pen-jing," or potted scenery.

 A simple but dramatic composition using three small Chinese junipers on a piece of rock is demonstrated here. The scene is intended to remind the viewer of a distant mountain on which pine trees grow. An upright piece of rock is selected to give the composition its height, and the little twisted junipers are reminiscent of the gnarled old pines that grow in the high mountains shrouded in mist. The technical processes are simple and involve no high-tech gadgetry. Rather, it is the artistic choice of rock and plants that makes the miniature landscape so effective. It is surprising what you can do with a little bit of imagination.

❶ This rock is volcanic and is therefore light and porous. It is moisture retentive, and moss grows easily on it. We begin by selecting the face that is most attractive to use as the front of the composition. There are three natural platforms on which the junipers can be planted. Holes are drilled into the rock on the shelves where the trees are to be placed.

❷ After drilling the holes, copper or aluminum wires are inserted into the holes and cemented into place using epoxy resin. Make sure that the wire ends are long enough to be used for tying the root balls into their permanent positions. On each shelf, two to three pairs of wires are glued into position.

❸ The next step is to prepare a mixture of clay and peat, as shown here. The clay should have the consistency of sticky caramel or thick molasses so that it can be used like a cement mortar to hold the little trees in place.

4 Select the trees so that each one fits snugly into the platform on which it is to grow. The lean and twist of each tree should complement its position on the rock.

5 When you are satisfied that the tree you have chosen suits the position on the rock, tie the wire ends tightly to secure the tree into place. Use the sticky clay mixture to cement the tree to the rock.

6 Fill in all the crevices with the clay mixture so that the surface of the soil blends in with the rock. The surface can now be planted with fine moss to give the impression that the trees have been growing on the rock for years. The more natural the composition looks, the more convincing it will be.

The finished composition is of ancient pines clinging to a rocky precipice. To the ancient Chinese, this was a symbol of man's struggle for survival against adversity. For them, bonsai was not simply about growing miniature trees—it was very much a visual, intellectual, and spiritual experience.

TAXUS PROJECT

No book on bonsai would be complete without some reference to the creation and use of driftwood. Driftwood effects are extremely popular today, due mainly to the inspirational work of Masahiko Kimura. Driftwood is not new to bonsai; it has been used for centuries because it is a natural feature on many bonsai collected from the wild.

 Driftwood effects, or "jins and sharis," are mostly used on evergreen conifers such as Chinese juniper, needle juniper, pine, yew, and spruce. These species are often found in the wild, complete with natural driftwood. Bonsai artists who are good at carving can produce driftwood effects that are equally spectacular. In this example, we show how a large Japanese yew *(Taxus cuspidata)* is transformed from an ordinary bonsai into an exquisite piece of living sculpture.

❶ This tree had to be nursed back to health by growing it in a large pot filled with sphagnum moss. Once the tree was sufficiently strong, the two lower branches were made into "jins," and only the leader was allowed to continue growing.

❷ The branches that grew from the leader were used to make the triangular outline of the tree. The leader was bent back on itself with heavy guy wires to make the tree more compact. Next, the leader was bent back even more to emphasize the triangular outline of the tree and allow the bends to merge with the curvature of the trunk. This was done by splitting the trunk with a trunk-splitting tool and then wrapping raffia around it so that it could be bent and shaped without the risk of breakage.

❸ Once the desired shape was achieved, the next stage in the process was to use guy wires to hold it firmly in place.

The same tree immediately after carving and restyling. This tree will be ready for displaying at major exhibitions in about two years' time.

4 To protect the foliage from damage while carving driftwood, the greenery is wrapped in plastic. Protective gear is worn to shield the face from flying debris.

5 Sand down rough edges with sandpaper or a fine buffing tool. Using a nylon or brass wire brush, wash the wood down with clean water, then allow it to dry. Apply the lime sulfur with a soft paintbrush—do this in the shade so that it dries slowly. In direct sunlight, it will dry too quickly and turn yellow. A few applications may be needed to get the right color.

6 Remove the protective cloth. We can now study the form and structure of the branches and decide how best to prune before the final wiring. Each foliage pad is pruned in herringbone fashion in readiness for the final wiring. It is only after wiring that the finished shape will emerge.

7 Thick branches are wrapped in raffia to facilitate bending. The tree is now left to grow until the spring when it will be repotted at the correct angle. The wire will be left on the tree for at least two or three years for the shape to set.

DISPLAYING AND EXHIBITING

Bonsai are works of art and deserve to be properly displayed, whether at home as part of a private collection or in a public exhibition. There are many ways of displaying bonsai: one's own collection is best displayed in a tasteful garden setting, while individual trees at exhibitions are best shown as if in an art gallery setting.

Most bonsai exhibitions follow in the Japanese tradition, where individual trees are displayed in 4-foot (1.3-m) wide bays on traditional bonsai stands and with an "accent" plant or viewing stone as a contrasting accessory for each tree.

In the Japanese home, the tokonoma, or alcove, is used as the display setting for a beautiful bonsai to remind the viewer of the season. Each display usually features a tree or plant that typifies that time of the year. In spring, a spring flowering tree will be shown, while in the fall, a tree with autumn color will take center stage. A tokonoma display has three elements—the bonsai, a scroll, and the companion object, which may be a small plant, or suiseki, or viewing stone.

A traditional tokonoma display featuring the three elements of bonsai, scroll, and accent planting.

ABOVE A nursery at Syunkaen, where some of the finest bonsai in Japan are displayed in an exquisite setting.

BELOW The author's famous Japanese mountain maple, which has been in his collection for 30 years. Here it is displayed in a formal setting at the world-famous Chelsea Flower Show in London, England.

SECRETS OF SUCCESS

Bonsai should never be displayed on the ground. Place them individually on stands or benches so that they are at waist- or eye-level. Keep the display area neat and tidy at all times to enhance the presentation and to reduce the risk of pests and diseases.

9

TROUBLESHOOTING AND HEALTH PROBLEMS

*"By tending and caring for your bonsai,
you form a symbiotic relationship with nature."*

COMMON PROBLEMS

Like all living organisms, plants can suffer from bad health. The three main causes of plant health problems are pests, diseases, and disorders. However careful you are with your bonsai, problems can arise. The key to success lies in being able to recognize the symptoms, identify the cause, and use the right cure.

 The signs of poor plant health tend to be obvious. The color and texture of the foliage are the first things to check. If the leaves or needles are beginning to turn yellow when they should be green, you need to investigate further. If the plant is limp and the leaves droop for no apparent reason, something is seriously wrong.

The cause of a tree's poor health is very often found in its roots. Examine them carefully by taking the tree out of its pot. Roots can be damaged in a number of ways, including dehydration, saturation, and attack by pests or a disease. When a bonsai's roots cannot function normally, the leaves receive an inadequate supply of water and nutrients, which makes them go limp or drop off.

Pests and diseases

Leaf damage is usually caused by pests or disease. Fungal diseases and mineral deficiencies show up as unusual leaf pigmentation. However, invaders are not easy to identify. Scale insect, white fly, and red spider mite are not easily visible. In these cases, you can only trace the infestation via the symptoms.

Recognizing when there's a problem is the key to good plant health management. Observe each bonsai carefully when you water. If you can identify a problem at the outset, you will have a better chance of a successful cure. A healthy tree has plump and healthy foliage with no blemishes. Sick trees invariably have lackluster foliage and dead twigs. Dead twigs are often caused by inadequate light.

Blotchy leaves on *Zelkova serrata* caused by using excessively strong insecticide; poor air circulation encourages fluffy scale; browning tips of beech leaves due to bad watering.

SUMMER

ALL TYPES OF TREES

Symptom	Causes	Remedies	Preventative measures
Leaves become dry and shrivel up but the bark shows green when scratched.	Forgetting to water for a few days.	Cut off all the dry leaves, water, and place the tree in shade. New leaves will grow in about a month. Don't feed the tree immediately after cutting the leaves; wait a month until the tree is growing strongly again.	Water regularly. Arrange for someone to water for you if you cannot or invest in an automatic watering system.
Tips of leaves shrivel up.	Insecticide damage.	Cut off all the damaged leaves so that a new crop will grow or let the leaves fall naturally.	As above. Don't spray in strong sunshine or use chemicals at too concentrated a solution. If the sun is too strong, consider using a shade structure in summer.
	Watering in strong sunshine.	Water morning and evening only.	Consider using a shade structure in the summer to protect trees against strong sun.
Curled up or blotchy leaves.	Pest infestation or fungal disease. Could also be insecticide damage.	Identify the pest or fungal disease and spray with an appropriate chemical. Cut off all the leaves and wait for new leaves to grow.	Monitor the health of your bonsai carefully. The sooner you take action against pests and diseases, the less damage they will do. Don't use insecticide at too concentrated a strength.

SPRING

DECIDUOUS TREES

Symptom	Causes	Remedies	Preventative measures
Tree shows no sign of life: bark is no longer green when scratched. It is brown or cream colored.	Tree was not repotted earlier in the spring. Entire tree or roots may have been damaged by frost; waterlogging due to poor drainage; insufficient watering.	None—the tree has died.	Protect bonsai over winter in a sheltered spot or in an unheated greenhouse. Water regularly so that the root ball is kept damp but not soaking wet.
No sign of life, although tree has been repotted.	The roots that were cut during repotting may have been damaged by frost.	As above.	Protect bonsai over winter in a sheltered spot or in an unheated greenhouse.
Tree shows no sign of life, but the bark shows green when scratched.	Roots damaged by frost, waterlogging, or insufficient watering.	Remove half the soil from the root ball. Cut out any rotten roots and plant the tree in a deep pot using sphagnum moss or an open free-draining medium. Apply some vitamin B solution or one of the proprietary Japanese reviving fluids; then water moderately to keep the soil just damp until the tree recovers.	Protect bonsai from hard frost in a shed or unheated greenhouse. Water regularly so that the root ball is kept damp but not soaking wet.
Tree begins to leaf, but the leaves quickly shrivel up.	Root rot or insecticide damage.	Plant in sphagnum moss or a medium with an open mix, as above. If the bark shows green when scratched, new leaves will grow in time.	Protect trees from drafts and frost when new leaves emerge. Avoid spraying fungicide or insecticide on trees when the leaves are still soft; wait until they harden. If you have to spray, use the chemical at half-strength.

SPRING (CONTINUED)

EVERGREEN TREES

Symptom	Causes	Remedies	Preventative measures
Foliage gradually turns yellow and then brown.	Could be frost damage or root rot caused by waterlogging. New roots may have been damaged in repotting.	Plant in sphagnum moss or a medium with an open mix.	Protect evergreens from frost by moving them to shelter. Water regularly and keep them out of drafts. Take the trees outside when the weather turns mild. Newly potted trees should be tied firmly so that they don't rock in the wind. Beware: evergreens can take a long time to show signs of distress. Try to spot symptoms early.

YELLOWING LEAVES
ON EUGENIA

FROST DAMAGE
ON CELTIS

FALL/WINTER

CONIFERS AND TENDER TROPICAL SPECIES

Symptom	Causes	Remedies	Preventative measures
Conifer needles start to turn yellow.	The tree is healthy. Old needles turn yellow and drop at this time of the year.	Remove any old needles from the branches that don't fall naturally.	None required.
White fluffy insects on conifer needles.	Adelgids *(see page 160)*.	Spray with insecticide.	Infestation cannot be prevented. Be vigilant and treat when necessary.
Leaf blackening (tender tropical species).	Frost damage.	The damage cannot be undone. A vulnerable tree is unlikely to recover.	Keep trees protected from frost.

PESTS

Insect pests are part of nature's rich biodiversity, but they can be a nuisance if allowed to proliferate unchecked. In recent years, the authorities have become more environmentally aware and now carefully control pesticide use. But sometimes, despite our best intentions to be environmentally friendly, organic methods are not effective and one has to resort to chemical means.

ADELGIDS

Easily confused with woolly aphids, these insects are also covered with a white, woolly substance. They prey mainly on pines, larch, and spruce, and are rarely found on other species. Japanese white pine and Scots pine are favorite host plants. Adelgids are very destructive because they are sap-sucking insects. They appear mainly in spring, but are active throughout the year. Constant vigilance and the application of insecticide are necessary for proper control.

ADELGIDS ON PINE

APHIDS ON MAPLE

APHIDS

Commonly known as greenfly and blackfly, aphids are found on new soft shoots and the leaves of deciduous trees, maples in particular. They also prey on Satsuki azaleas. Indoor trees such as elm, *Sageretia, Serissa, Ficus, Carmona,* and *Celtis* are also susceptible. Systemic and nonsystemic insecticides are both suitable. Malathion is effective but can blacken the young leaves of deciduous trees. Insecticides containing bifenthrin are much kinder to young leaves. A light spray during the winter will kill any eggs.

RED SPIDER MITE

Usually found in warm conditions, especially on indoor trees, red spider mites are hard to spot because they are so tiny (up to $\frac{1}{25}$ inch /1 mm long). They form colonies on the undersides of leaves. Check for infestation by holding a piece of white paper under a branch and shaking it. Red spider mite is difficult to eradicate with insecticide, although malathion should control the problem. You can also try washing the mites off with a hose. Leaving the infected tree outside for a few days can also be effective.

RED SPIDER MITE ON CACTUS

ALB DAMAGE TO TREE

ASIAN LONG-HORNED BEETLE (ALB)

ALB is one of the most dangerous pests in North America and Europe, and has the potential to destroy many of the Western hemisphere's hardwood forests. Its native habitat is China and Japan, but it has entered the West in the last decade via wood-packaging material and illegal plant importation. ALB has already been spotted in some of our forests. The bonsai community has a responsibility to watch for this pest and kill it as soon as it is seen. ALB is easy to identify, because it grows up to 1½ inches (4 cm) long. It has a shiny black surface, with prominent white spots and long antennae. It preys on deciduous trees, especially maples. The female lays eggs in the bark, and the grubs that hatch tunnel into the heartwood, while the adult insects chew on the bark and leaves. Infestation is usually identified by the larvae's exit holes, which are about ¼ inch (6 mm) in diameter and have a sprinkling of sawdust at their base.

SCALE INSECTS

There are many forms of scale insect—the most common are white or brown, waxy creatures that adhere to the undersides of leaves and twigs. Soft scale are found on the underside of broadleaf trees such as maples and *Ficus*. Their sticky excrement encourages sooty mold. Most insecticides control soft scale. If the infestation is light, you can squash them with paper or apply wood alcohol. Brown or hemispherical scale are usually found on evergreens such as elaeagnus and camellia bonsai. Control can be effective if you spot the problem early, while the scales are still young. Juniper scale or mites are tiny, white, scalelike insects that prey on Chinese and needle juniper and sometimes yew. They can be controlled with insecticide.

SCALE INSECTS ON MAPLE

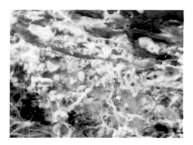

ROOT APHIDS ON PINE

ROOT APHIDS

Root aphids resemble black fly, but are white and prey on the roots of many tree species, such as pine and beech. These trees usually have a beneficial fungus called mycorrhizae in their roots, which is easily confused with a root-aphid infestation, so carry out a close examination with a magnifying glass. If you identify an infestation, soak the root ball in insecticide or apply as a spray.

VINE WEEVIL

VINE WEEVIL GRUBS

In recent years, the vine weevil has become one of the most trouble-some pests in Europe. They are particularly fond of maples, camellias, azaleas, and rhododendrons, as well as pines and junipers. The adult beetle lays its eggs in the soil during the summer, and it is the larvae that cause the most damage because they eat away at a plant's roots. Chemicals such as permethrin can control the larvae. Biological control methods that use the tiny parasitic nematodes are also very effective and are now widely available for amateur gardeners. The time at which you apply nematodes is crucial and should coincide with the hatching of the eggs in late summer. The adults appear only at night, to feed, and you can use this opportunity to hunt them down. You can also eradicate any grubs in the root ball when you repot your bonsai in spring.

LEAF DAMAGE

VINE WEEVIL

WOOLLY APHIDS

These insects are covered with a white woolly wax and prey mainly on the bark of deciduous trees, where they suck the sap. They are very unsightly, and the sticky substance they leave behind can serve as a substrate for the sooty mold. You can eradicate them by squashing them with a piece of cloth or paper. Alternatively, use a systemic insecticide to poison them when they suck the sap from host plant. Ordinary contact insecticide is ineffective because the woolly covering on this pest offers them a lot of protection. There are also predator insects that you can use.

WOOLLY APHID

WHITE FLY

WHITE FLY

White fly are small sap-sucking insects that are usually found in warm, humid conditions, such as in a greenhouse. They prey mainly on indoor bonsai, on the undersides of leaves. They attack most species of plants and are easy to spot because they fly around when disturbed. The tell-tale sign is yellow spots on the leaves, which tend to fall off. White fly may also promote sooty mold on the twigs and branches. Use an insecticide or insect traps—these are strips of sticky yellow paper that you place near the tree to trap the insects when they fly around.

TREE SPECIES AND COMMON PESTS

Abies	aphids, adelgids, and vine weevil
Acer	aphids, scale insects (soft and fluffy scale), caterpillars, Asian long-horned beetle, and vine weevil
Azalea	aphids, white fly, and vine weevil
Camellia	soft scale and vine weevil
Carpinus	scale insects
Cedrus	spider mites
Chaenomeles	aphids
Chamaecyparis	spider mites and vine weevil
Cotoneaster	aphids, scale insects, and woolly aphids
Crataegus	aphids, sawfly, and caterpillars
Fagus	scale insects, woolly aphids, and vine weevil
Fraxinus	scale insects
Ilex	aphids and scale insects
Juniperus	aphids, scale insects, and mites
Laburnum	slugs
Larix	adelgids
Malus	aphids, caterpillars, and woolly aphids
Morus	scale insects and spider mites
Picea	adelgids, aphids, and spider mites
Pinus	adelgids, spider mites, and caterpillars
Prunus	aphids and scale insects
Pyracantha	aphids, scale insects, and woolly aphids
Quercus	scale insects and caterpillars
Rosa	scale insects, caterpillars, and vine weevil
Salix	aphids, scale insects, and caterpillars
Taxus	scale insects and vine weevil
Ulmus	scale insects, white fly, and red spider mite
Wisteria	aphids, scale insects, and vine weevil

OTHER PLANT PREDATORS

CATERPILLARS

Caterpillars can strip all the leaves off a tree—they are fond of new leaves and shoots. Some caterpillars bore into the stems of trees, so the damage may not be visible. Control them by destroying them physically or by spraying with an insecticide.

RODENTS

Small rodents damage the bark and shoots of trees, and may also knock over and physically damage the bonsai. Rabbits and squirrels often plague professional growers who cultivate trees in the open ground. A close-mesh galvanized wire netting or fencing is effective at keeping them away.

SLUGS AND SNAILS

Slugs are voracious feeders and can cause a lot of damage to young plants. They are particularly fond of laburnum, wisteria, and hosta. They hide under bonsai pots and sometimes inside the pot itself. Control them with slug pellets.

DISEASES

Plants, like humans, are prone to disease. General cleanliness will reduce the risk of infection considerably. Diseases in plants are caused by bacteria, viruses, and fungi. Since many of these organisms can be transmitted by insects, animals, humans, or by air and water, vigilance is important. Identifying the disease is the first step in controlling its spread.

CORAL SPOT

This disease is easily recognized by the bright orange spots that form on a tree's branches and trunk. It is most commonly seen on Japanese maples, although some elms, such as *Zelkova serrata*, are also susceptible. It is a fungal disease that is spread easily by pruning implements and by water splashing on the orange pustules. The best way to deal with this disease is to cut out the affected portions out and burn them. Always disinfect your pruning tools after use.

CORAL SPOT ON JAPANESE MAPLE

DAMPING-OFF ON SEEDLINGS

DAMPING-OFF

Damping-off is a fungal disease. It affects seedlings and is similar to root rot. Infected seedlings suddenly wilt and die for no apparent reason. You can use Bordeaux mixture to prevent this disease, but good hygiene and avoiding overwatering are better ways to manage it. If you germinate your seedlings in a greenhouse or an enclosed propagator, providing good ventilation at an early stage—for example, as soon as the seedlings have germinated—can reduce damping-off quite considerably.

FIREBLIGHT

This disease affects the Rosaceae family. The symptoms are sudden blackening of the leaves and stems and cankerous growth on the branches. It is an airborne, bacterial disease that is very difficult to eradicate. Bonsai that are susceptible to this disease are cotoneaster, crab apple, pyracantha, and hawthorn. As soon as the symptoms appear, you should cut out the infected twigs or branches and burn them immediately to prevent the bacteria from spreading.

FIREBLIGHT ON APPLE BRANCH

GALLS

Many types of galls affect bonsai. Some, such as azalea galls, found on Satsuki azaleas, affect the leaves. Others affect the plant stems. If you discover the symptoms, cut off the affected portion and burn it. Spraying with Bordeaux mixture or copper fungicide may also help. Galls spread easily when there is poor ventilation. With azaleas it is a good idea to stand them on well-ventilated benches and leave plenty of space between them.

GALL ON SATSUKI AZALEA

ROOT ROT ON CHAMAECYPARIS

ROOT ROT

Root rots are fungal diseases that mainly attack conifers such as juniper, pine, and *Chamaecyparis*, although maples may also be affected. Once a plant is infected, there is little you can do. The roots suffer first, but the disease spreads rapidly to other parts of the tree and you may not discover the disease until the foliage turns brown. If root rot is detected early enough, you can try to save the tree by planting it in sphagnum moss. Avoid root rot by watering vulnerable trees sparingly. Good soil drainage also helps.

RUST AND BLACK SPOT

Plants that belong to the Rosaceae family, such as hawthorn, cotoneaster, pyrancantha, crab apple, *Prunus*, and *Sorbus*, are particularly suscep-tible to rust. The symptoms usually appear in midsummer, when the leaves may turn yellow and drop prematurely. Black spot can also be a problem for these plants. Chemicals like Bordeaux mixture are very effective at controlling both diseases. Affected leaves should be gathered and burned immediately to prevent the disease from spreading.

RUST ON HAWTHORN

VERTICILLIUM WILT ON JAPANESE MAPLE

VERTICILLIUM WILT

This is a fungal disease that affects mainly maples, especially when they are growing in the ground. A diseased trunk or branch that has been cut through will reveal characteristic dark, vertical stripes, which run through the wood. Verticillium wilt is very difficult to control. Fortunately, it seldom affects maples in pots. If you grow maples in the open ground and find that your plants are affected, do not replant in the same position. Disinfect the soil where the affected plant was growing and burn the dead tree.

10

PLANT DIRECTORY

"The fact that your tree can never be finished is part of the adventure and mystery of bonsai."

INDOOR VARIETIES

The varieties of bonsai that you can grow indoors will depend on the growing conditions that you can provide for the plants. In addition to the temperature, the light levels and humidity are critical factors. Always remember that most of the so-called "indoor" varieties are outdoor plants in their native habitat. Getting them to grow successfully indoors involves a great deal of patience and experimentation.

EASY INDOOR VARIETIES

The following species are all suitable for average living-room conditions: 60°–75°F (15°–23°C):

- *Aralia* (most varieties)
- *Crassula* (Jade tree)
- *Cycas revoluta*
- *Euphorbia* (most varieties)
- *Ficus benjamina* (Weeping fig), both green and variegated types
- *Ficus* "Long Island"
- *Ficus natalensis*
- *Ficus microcarpa nitida*
- *Hedera* (Ivy)
- *Schefflera* (*Brassaia actinophylla* and dwarf *Schefflera* varieties)
- Succulents (most varieties)
- *Ulmus parvifolia* (Chinese elm from southern China)

COOL INDOOR VARIETIES

Optimum temperature: 45°–60°F (7°–15°C)

- *Acacia dealbata* (Mimosa)
- *Azalea indicum*
- *Buxus* (Boxwood)
- *Camellia*
- *Celtis* (most varieties)
- Citrus varieties
- *Cotoneaster microphyllus*
- Cypress
- *Ficus carica* (Common edible fig)
- *Fortunella*
- *Fuchsia* (hardy varieties)
- *Gardenia*
- *Hedera* (Ivy)
- Junipers (certain tropical and subtropical varieties)
- *Leptospermum*
- *Ligustrum* (both the Chinese and Japanese privet)
- *Lonicera nitida* (Hedging honeysuckle)
- *Myrtus* (myrtle)
- *Nandina domestica* (Heavenly bamboo)
- *Olea* (Olive)
- *Pinus halepensis* (Aleppo pine)
- *Pistacia*
- *Pyracantha* (Firethorn)
- *Punica* (Pomegranate)
- *Rhododendron simsii*
- *Rosmarinus* (Wild rosemary)
- *Taxodium distichum* (Bald cypress)
- *Trachelospermum jasminoides*
- *Ulmus parvifolia* (Chinese elm from southern China)

EXOTIC TROPICAL VARIETIES

To grow the following successfully, you need to create the right growing conditions artificially, using equipment to raise the temperature, humidity, and light levels. Optimum temperature: 65°–80°F (18°–26°C)

- *Bougainvillea glabra*
- *Bucida spinosa*
- *Buxus harlandii*
- *Calliandra* (Powderpuff tree)
- *Casuarina equisetifolia*
- *Conocarpus erectus* (buttonwood)
- *Cuphea hyssopifolia* (Mexican heather)
- *Ehretia buxifolia* (also called *Carmona retusa* or Fujian tea)
- *Eugenia*

- *Ficus benghalensis*
- *Ficus citrifolia brevifolia*
- *Ficus deltoidia var. diversifolia*
- *Ficus virens*
- *Ficus microcarpa*
- *Ficus nerifolia*
- *Ficus pumila*
- *Ficus religiosa*
- *Hibiscus*
- *Jacaranda*
- *Lagerstroemia* (Crape myrtle)
- *Lantana*
- *Malpighia coccigera* (Barbados cherry)

- *Murraya paniculata* (Orange jessamine)
- *Phempis acidula*
- *Podocarpus macrophyllus* (Maki or Buddha pine)
- *Polyscias* (Ming aralia)
- *Rhapis humilus* (Rhapis palm)
- *Sageretia theezans* (Chinese bird plum cherry)
- *Serissa foetida* (Tree of a thousand stars)
- *Syzygium*

(These varieties are the true tropicals and very few bonsai specialists will stock them. They are normally available only by special order.)

CRASSULA (JADE TREE)

CHINESE ELM

OUTDOOR VARIETIES

Despite the increasing interest in indoor bonsai, the hobby remains firmly rooted in the outdoor tradition. The vast majority of bonsai enthusiasts grow outdoor trees because this is how bonsai should really be grown. By choosing the species that grow well in your climate, you should have years of pleasure from your bonsai. The list that follows is intended for those who live in temperate regions. For those living in the tropics, the indoor varieties can be grown outdoors.

CONIFERS

The following conifers make suitable bonsai in temperate regions:

- *Abies* (silver firs—*A. firma, A. koreana, A. lasiocarpa, A. sachlinensis*)
- *Cedrus* (cedars—*C. atlantica, C. deodara, C. libani*)
- *Chamaecyparis obtusa* (Hinoki cypress—most varieties)
- *Chamaecyparis pisifera* (Sawara cypress— most varieties)

- *Cryptomeria japonica* (most varieties)
- *Ginkgo biloba*
- *Juniperus* (junipers— *J. californica, J. chinensis* in many varieties, *J. communis, J. conferta, J. x media* in many varieties, *J. procumbens, J. rigida, J. squamata, J. virginiana*)
- *Larix* (larch—*L. decidua, L. kaempferi*)
- *Metasequoia glyptostroboides* (Dawn redwood)
- *Picea* (spruces—*P. abies, P. glauca, P. jezoensis, P. orientalis*)
- *Pinus* (pines—*P. aristata, P. densiflora, P. mugo, P. nigra, P. parviflora, P. rigida, P. strobus, P. sylvestris, P. thunbergii*)

HINOKI CYPRESS

- *Sequoia* (redwoods— *S. sempervirens*)
- *Sequoiadendron giganteum* (Giant redwood or Wellingtonia)
- *Taxodium distichum* (Swamp cypress)
- *Taxus* (yew—*T. baccata, T. cuspidata*)

CEDRUS

OTHER TREES AND SHRUBS

The following deciduous varieties do well as bonsai in temperate climates:

- *Acer buergerianum* (trident maple)
- *Acer palmatum* and *A. japonicum* (Japanese maples, many varieties)
- *Acer campestre* (Hedge maple)
- *Acer tatarium sspiginnala* (Amur maple)
- *Aesculus* (horse chestnuts and buckeyes)
- *Alnus* (Alders)
- *Amelanchier* (Juneberry or serviceberry)
- *Azalea* (most species, but in particular, the Satsuki azalea)
- *Berberis* (most species)
- *Betula* (birch)
- *Buxus* (box)
- *Camellia*
- *Caragana* (Chinese pea tree)
- *Carpinus* (hornbeam—European Japanese and Korean species)
- *Cercis (canadensis* and *siliquastrum)*
- *Chaenomeles* (ornamental quince)
- *Cornus (mas* and *officinalis)*
- *Corylus* (hazel or filbert tree)
- *Cotinus*
- *Cotoneaster (horizontalis* and other small-leaf varieties)

- *Crataegus* (hawthorns, most varieties)
- *Cydonia* (Chinese quince)
- *Elaeagnus* (most varieties)
- *Escallonia*
- *Euonymus* (spindle tree)
- *Fagus* (ash—European and Japanese species)
- *Forsythia*
- *Hedera* (ivy, most varieties)
- *Ilex (aquifolium, crenata,* and *serrata)*
- *Laburnum*
- *Ligustrum* (privet)
- *Liquidambar*
- *Lonicera (morrowii*—Japanese honeysuckle and *nitida*—hedging honeysuckle)
- *Magnolia (stellata* and *liliflora)*
- *Malus* (Crab apple, most varieties)
- *Morus* (mulberry—red and white)
- *Nothofagus* (Southern beech)
- *Potentilla*
- *Prunus* (most varieties)
- *Pyracantha*
- *Quercus* (oak species)
- *Rhododendron* (small-leaf varieties)

- *Salix* (willows—weeping varieties)
- *Sophora*
- *Sorbus*
- *Spirea*
- *Stephanandra*
- *Tamarix*
- *Ulmus* (elms, in particular *crassifolia, parvifolia,* and *pumila)*
- *Viburnum*
- Wisteria (most varieties)
- *Zelkova* (Japanese gray bark elm)

PINK WISTERIA

JAPANESE MAPLE

GLOSSARY

air layering A method of vegetative propagation used extensively for producing fairly mature plants in a relatively short space of time. It uses the plant's inherent ability to produce roots from the trunk or branch by burying or covering that part with soil or other rooting material.

Akadama Japanese bonsai soil produced from processed red clay granules.

approach grafting A method of grafting new branches on bonsai in the precise location where they are needed. It is achieved by bringing a branch of the same or another tree into direct contact with the trunk after cutting into the cambium layer and tightly joining the two together.

bonsai Plant or tree grown in a special container and kept miniature by restricting its roots and by pruning the branches into an artistic shape to resemble a fully grown tree in nature.

Chinese bonsai A genre of bonsai created by Chinese bonsai artists that is typically stylized and resembles the images of trees in classical Chinese paintings. They have a less natural appearance than Japanese-style bonsai.

collected bonsai Bonsai created from material originally growing in the wild, often referred to in Japanese as Yama-dori bonsai or bonsai from the mountains.

driftwood effects Dead wood on bonsai that may be natural or artificially created and is bleached white to resemble driftwood.

grafting A method of plant propagation invented by the Chinese more than two millennia ago in which a desired variety is joined to a suitable root stock in order to produce a plant with the characteristics of the variety.

in-arch grafting This is synonymous with approach grafting, but the term is usually used when the branch being grafted is from the same tree.

Japanese bonsai A genre of bonsai created by Japanese bonsai artists in which the trees have a more natural-looking appearance than those in the Chinese tradition.

jins Japanese term for dead wood on the tips of branches on a bonsai.

Literati (or Bunjin) style Style of bonsai created by literary scholars in ancient China that is characterized by tall, sparse-looking trees. It is reminiscent of Chinese calligraphy and brush-stroke paintings. Bunjin refers to the men of culture in the Edo period who were avid followers of Chinese art and literature, including bonsai.

nebari Japanese term for the surface roots around the base of a bonsai.

pen-jing The two words literally mean bonsai in the Chinese language, although in the modern context it refers to the miniature landscape-style of bonsai practiced by the Chinese.

potensai An expression that has come to be used in the West in recent years to denote plant material that has the potential to be trained into a bonsai.

Raft style A group of trees trained to resemble a forest made from a single plant that has been laid on its side.

sabi Japanese aesthetic term used to denote loneliness and solitude, invariably used in conjunction with the term "wabi."

shari Japanese term for the exposed dead wood on the trunk of a bonsai that is usually white in appearance.

shohin Japanese term for small bonsai, usually something that can be held in one hand, around 6–8 inches (15–20 cm) high.

wabi Japanese aesthetic term that means poverty, with elements of simplicity and contentment. It is usually used with the word "sabi."

wiring The process of applying metal wires on the trunks and/or branches of bonsai to create a desired configuration or shape.

RESOURCES

American Bonsai Society
www.absbonsai.org
National bonsai organization for
North America, including Mexico,
the United States, and Canada.
A variety of educational and support
services, information and links
to other sites.

Bonsai in Australia
www.geocities.com/Tokyo/Palace/7574/
australia.html
Links to bonsai clubs in Australia and
New Zealand and other useful bonsai
Web sites.

Bonsai Network Japan
www.J-bonsai.com/
Bonsai tours and more in Japan.

Bonsai Talk
www.bonsaitalk.com/
A free Internet community devoted to
the advancement of the arts of bonsai.

The Bonsaisite.com Network
network.bonsaisite.com/
A list of regional bonsai clubs, bonsai
nurseries online, plus info, supplies,
and links to other sites.

Herons Bonsai
Wiremill Lane
Newchapel
Nr Lingfield
Surrey RH7 6HJ
Phone: +44 1342 832657
Fax: +44 1342 832025
www.herons.co.uk
Britain's premier bonsai nursery,
owned by Peter Chan.

Mid-America Bonsai Alliance
www.wwnet/~scott13/maba.html

MidAtlantic Bonsai Societies
midatlanticbonsai.freeservers.com/

The National Bonsai Foundation
www.bonsai-nbf.org/
Supporting the National Bonsai and
Penjing Museum at the U.S. National
Arboretum. Museum collections, plus
bonsai information and links.

North American Bonsai Federation
www.bonsai-wbff.org/nabf/main.htm
NABF carries out the mission of the
World Bonsai Friendship Federation
(WBFF) to foster peace, friendship,
and goodwill in the world through
bonsai and related art forms. Through
this website, NABF will keep you
informed of its activities as it seeks
to strengthen the bonsai community
in North America.

FURTHER READING

Bonsai
Peter Chan
(Thunder Bay Press, 2002)

**Bonsai: The Art of Growing
and Keeping Miniature Trees**
Peter Chan *(Book Sales, 2001)*

Bonsai Masterclass
Peter Chan *(Sterling, 1993)*

INDEX